At Issue

| Heroin

Other books in the At Issue series:

At Issue

| Heroin

Stuart A. Kallen, Book Editor

GREENHAVEN PRESS
An imprint of Thomson Gale, a part of The Thomson Corporation

THOMSON
━━━━★━━━━ ™
GALE

Detroit • New York • San Francisco • New Haven, Conn. • Waterville, Maine • London

Bonnie Szumski, *Publisher*
Helen Cothran, *Managing Editor*

LIBRARY OF CONGRESS CATALOGING-IN-PUBLICATION DATA

Heroin / Stuart A. Kallen, book editor.
    p. cm. -- (At issue)
  Includes bibliographical references and index.
    ISBN 0-7377-2715-2 (lib. hardcover : alk. paper) -- ISBN 0-7377-2716-0 (pbk. : alk. paper)
    1. Heroin abuse. 2. Heroin abuse--United States. 3. Heroin abuse--Treatment. 4. Drug addicts--Rehabilitation. 5. Drug control--United States. I. Kallen, Stuart A., 1955– II. Series: At issue (San Diego, Calif.)
    HV5822.H4H455 2007
    362.29'3--dc22

                                                    2006017516

Printed in the United States of America
10 9 8 7 6 5 4 3 2 1

Contents

Introduction

Known alternatively as smack, H, China white, skag, horse, and black tar, heroin is commonly considered to be among the most dangerous, addictive, and deadly drugs in the world. Even casual users can become addicted to heroin, and those who habitually use the drug face countless negative consequences. Part of its harmful image is reflected in one of the drug's most enduring nicknames—junk. Addicts, or junkies, who try to stop taking heroin undergo physical withdrawal symptoms that are among the most horrible afflictions a person can experience.

Because of the well-known dangers associated with the drug, heroin use is not widespread in the United States. According to the National Survey on Drug Use and Health, only about 314,000 people over the age of twelve used heroin in 2003, while an estimated 2.4 million people have used the drug at some time in their lives. Although less than 1 percent of the population has taken the drug, heroin has generated a disproportionate amount of misery. According to the Drug Abuse Warning Network (DAWN), which collects data on drug-related hospital emergency incidents from twenty-one metropolitan areas, 14 percent of all drug-related emergency room episodes involved heroin.

Despite the known dangers, heroin continues to entice new users, some of whom see the drug as fashionable or chic. The attraction of "heroin chic," according to some young female users, is the physical appearance that heroin gives addicts. The physical trademarks of heroin chic include pale skin, dark circles underneath the eyes, and jutting bones like those seen on runway models. Others are attracted to heroin because of the inspired works created by junkies such as Nirvana frontman Kurt Cobain and renowned author and poet William S. Burroughs.

Whatever the initial attraction, novices commonly spiral into addiction because of the fast-acting, euphoric effects initially felt when taking the drug. These are described by a first-time user known only as Benjamin, who wrote about snorting heroin on the Erowid Experiences Vaults Web site:

> Heroin is like no other physical sensation I have ever felt. ... [No other drug has ever] blanketed my entire body with absolute, unadulterated GOODNESS for so long. Nothing outside of the heroin experience matters. The only world that exists is the small, warm and very, very comfortable bubble of pleasure that has enveloped your drooping human frame. ... When you're on heroin, you know that no-one feels as good as you do, and subsequently no-one else matters.

What Benjamin and other users find, however, is that the euphoria experienced by first-time users becomes impossible to achieve after repeated use. Addicts build up a tolerance to the drug, and those who began by snorting or smoking the powdered form of the drug find that they must take heroin intravenously in increasingly larger doses simply to feel normal. Without the drug, addicts experience extreme withdrawal discomforts, including vomiting, diarrhea, violent fits of sneezing, inability to catch one's breath, watering eyes, runny nose, intense itching, chills and goose bumps (hence the phrase, "cold turkey"), and involuntary muscle spasms that cause the legs to jerk (giving rise to the phrase "kicking the habit"). An anonymous writer on Erowid describes watching his uncle trying to kick the habit:

> It was the most disgusting thing I have ever seen. I sat there horrified as I watched him convulse and vomit up slime. His eyes rolled into the back of his head and he looked as if he were dead. The stench was worse than that of burning flesh. It was one of the most disgusting things I have ever seen in my entire life. I was terrified.

To prevent these violent physical symptoms, heroin users take extreme risks. To pay for the drug, addicts are often forced into lives of crime and prostitution. Buying the drug on the streets means that users risk injecting drugs into their veins that may be adulterated with talcum powder, strychnine, or even concrete. Users who share needles risk contracting HIV, hepatitis, and other infections. The dangers associated with addiction are spelled out in a study by the *American Journal of Public Health* that found that 28 percent of deaths among addicts were from violence, 17 percent were from natural causes, and 44 percent were drug related, either from overdosing or shooting adulterated drugs.

Although few would dispute the dangers faced by heroin addicts, some say the emotionally charged debate surrounding heroin is overblown. As renowned author and poet William S. Burroughs writes in his novel *Junky*, heroin is not as addictive as most people believe:

> It takes at least three months' shooting twice a day to get any habit at all. And you don't really know what junk sickness is until you have [kicked the habit and restarted drug use] several times. It took me almost six months to get my first habit, and then the withdrawal symptoms were mild. I think it is no exaggeration to say it takes a year and several hundred injections to make an addict.

If Burroughs is right, it remains a mystery why people expend great effort to become addicted to a drug that even few junkies would recommend. Whatever the case, society must deal with people who make such choices. The result has been an ongoing debate as to whether addicts should be jailed or supplied with untainted heroin, clean needles, or various drugs to maintain their habit while seeking treatment. The debate is far from settled, and the problems associated with heroin use will doubtless continue into the foreseeable future.

1

The U.S. Drug War in Afghanistan Is Reducing Opium Production

Michael A. Braun

Michael A. Braun is chief of operations for the U.S. Drug Enforcement Administration.

Farmers in Afghanistan produce nearly nine-tenths of the world's opium. This drug is then converted into heroin and sold in Europe, the United States, and elsewhere. Although democracy has been introduced in Afghanistan since the U.S. invasion in 2001, this positive development will be lost if opium production is allowed to continue. To combat the growing power of the narcotics trade, the Drug Enforcement Administration (DEA) has implemented an aggressive program to reduce opium production, destroy heroin labs, and arrest drug traffickers. With a strong antidrug presence in Afghanistan, the DEA is confident that the U.S. government can stop heroin production while simultaneously defunding terrorist groups that benefit from the drug trade.

The Drug Enforcement Administration (DEA) is keenly aware that the continued production of opium in Afghanistan is not only a significant threat to Afghanistan's future and the region's stability, but also could have worldwide

Michael A. Braun, "U.S. Counternarcotics Policy in Afghanistan: Time for Leadership," Committee on International Relations, House of Representatives, March 17, 2005. http://commdocs.house.gov/committees/intlrel/hfa20058.000/hfa20058_0.HTM#48.

implications. In response to this threat, the DEA has undertaken an aggressive approach to combat the production of opium in Afghanistan. . . . Our efforts, combined with those of our law enforcement partners, through a program known as Operation Containment, have resulted in significant opium and heroin seizures in the region. We are also providing training and assistance to law enforcement personnel in Afghanistan, and the DEA is directly involved in overseeing and advising U.S. Government and Afghan officials in counternarcotics programs and drug policy issues in Afghanistan. The DEA is confident that our efforts, along with those of our U.S. and foreign counterparts, will result in the reduction of drugs produced in Afghanistan, and will ultimately assist in the stabilization of Afghanistan and the region.

Opium Production in Afghanistan

Years of warfare, punctuated by the Soviet invasion and occupation throughout the 1980s and the civil strife of the 1990s, decimated Afghanistan's economic infrastructure. During this period, the drug trade unfortunately emerged as Afghanistan's largest source of income. In 2001, the Taliban [the former rulers of Afghanistan] banned the cultivation of opium, which temporarily resulted in a significant decrease in production, to an estimated 74 metric tons. However, since the collapse of the Taliban in 2001, production has increased substantially. Official U.S. Government estimates for 2004 indicate that Afghanistan had the potential to produce 4,950 metric tons [5456 tons] of oven-dried opium, up from 2,865 metric tons [3158 tons] in 2003, and 1,278 metric tons [1408 tons] produced in 2002. According to the United Nations Office on Drugs and Crime (UNODC), Afghanistan produced 87 percent of the world's illicit opium supply in 2004, up from 75 percent in 2003. But in spite of these cultivation projections, there was not a commensurate rise in total opium yields. This was due to drought, disease, and the inexperience of new "farmers," which depressed the total per hectare output of opium. Although opium cultivation will continue throughout 2005, early surveys suggest a possibly significant decrease in opium production.

Meanwhile, the [new Afghan] administration has announced that there will be 100 percent eradication in 2005. This sends a clear message to farmers and opium cultivators that no amount of opium production will be tolerated. At present, there are two concurrently operating eradication programs in Afghanistan. The first is a U.K. Government-supported Central Poppy Eradication Force (CPEF). CPEF is comprised of 500 security personnel and about 1,000 locally hired Afghans who travel throughout the country to conduct ground eradication. In 2004 CPEF managed to eradicate only about 4,000 hectares [9884 acres] because of internal management issues and security concerns (some poppy growers laid explosive booby traps in their fields; 4 eradicators were killed). In 2005, CPEF intends to travel to Nangarhar and Helmand Provinces to strike the densest growth regions. The other eradication program is the governor-led eradication program. Although this program appears to be fraught with corruption issues (there are reports some governors are allowing opium growth in some areas, while eradicating the fields of political opponents), all governors in 2005 have pledged to support President [Hamid] Karzai's eradication initiatives. The governors' eradication program hires local militia, farmers, and police to destroy poppy fields.

Opiates produced in Afghanistan are typically consumed or smuggled to markets within the region, and also are smuggled to markets in the West.

The U.S. Government led the discussion in 2004, encouraging aerial eradication. However, the Afghanistan government is against such an approach for the time being.

The Production and Smuggling of Heroin and Morphine

Laboratories in Afghanistan convert opium into morphine base, white heroin, or one of several grades of brown heroin. The large processing labs are primarily located in southern Afghanistan, with smaller laboratories located in other areas, including Nangarhar Province. In the past, many opium processing laboratories were located in Pakistan, particularly in the Northwest Frontier Province (NWFP). These laboratories relocated to Afghanistan, to be closer to the source of opium and to avoid increasing law enforcement actions by the Government of Pakistan.

Opiates produced in Afghanistan are typically consumed or smuggled to markets within the region, and also are smuggled to markets in the West, with the majority of the opiate products in Europe originating in Afghanistan. Some small quantities of heroin produced in Afghanistan are smuggled to the United States.

Afghan heroin is trafficked via many routes, with traffickers quickly adjusting smuggling routes based on law enforcement and political actions, not to mention weather-related events. Traffickers in Afghanistan primarily rely on vehicles and overland routes to move drug shipments out of the country. A number of reports have been received indicating that large convoys of well-armed passenger trucks (up to 60 or more vehicles) loaded with opiates have been driven across western Afghanistan into Iran. Large freight trucks, known as "jinga" trucks are also loaded with drugs and sent toward Pakistan, while smaller shipments of drugs are sent through the northern Afghanistan border with Tajikistan. Afghan traffickers have become adept at using sophisticated concealment methods, such as traps and hidden compartments to hide opium, morphine, and heroin.

Also, reports indicate that heroin shipments moving north from Afghanistan through the Central Asian States to Russia have increased. Tajikistan law enforcement agencies report that approximately 80 percent of their drug seizures in Central Asia are opiates. Tajikistan is a primary transshipment location for opiate shipments destined for Russia. While some of the heroin is used in Russia, a portion transits Russia to other consumer markets in Western and Eastern Europe. Afghan heroin also transits India en route to international markets and continues to be trafficked from Afghanistan through Pakistan, with seizures frequently reported at Pakistan's international airports. Some heroin is smuggled by sea on vessels leaving the port city of Karachi [the commercial hub of Pakistan].

Morphine base is transported overland through Pakistan and Iran, or directly to Iran from Afghanistan, and then into Turkey, where Turkey-based trafficking groups convert the morphine base to heroin prior to shipment to European and North American markets. Shipments of Afghan-produced morphine base are also sent by sea from Pakistan's Makran Coast. Smuggling routes north through the Central Asian States, then across the Caspian Sea and south into Turkey also are used.

Afghanistan produces no essential or precursor chemicals. Acetic anhydride (AA), which is the most commonly used acetylating agent in heroin processing, is smuggled into Afghanistan from Pakistan, India, the Central Asian States, China, and Europe. . . .

The DEA is expanding its presence in Afghanistan by permanently stationing additional Special Agents and Intelligence Analysts to enhance that country's counternarcotics capacity.

The Five Pillar Plan

The DEA has joined with coalition partners, the State Department, and the Department of Defense (DOD) in the

U.S. Embassy Kabul [Afghanistan's capital] Counternarcotics Implementation Plan. This "Five Pillar Plan" provides the DEA opportunities, as never before, to reduce heroin production in Afghanistan and contribute to the stabilization and rebuilding of this war-torn country. Our primary role in this plan falls under the "Interdiction Pillar," where DEA will assist with the goal of destroying clandestine labs and seizing precursor chemicals, opium, and opiate stockpiles. To achieve that goal, the DEA is expanding its presence in Afghanistan by permanently stationing additional Special Agents and Intelligence Analysts to enhance that country's counternarcotics capacity. The DEA also will continue lending its expertise by providing drug enforcement training to our counterparts in the Counternarcotics Police-Afghanistan (CNP-A). This effort will build Afghanistan's institutions of justice and strengthen internal counternarcotics capabilities. The other two DEA components of the "Interdiction Pillar" are the Foreign-deployed Advisory and Support Teams and Operation Containment.

DEA's Presence in Afghanistan

The DEA's Kabul Country Office [CO] reopened in February 2003, and it has made significant progress, while enduring difficult conditions. Security constraints, as well as other conditions in Afghanistan, initially severely limited our agents' movements and their ability to conduct traditional drug enforcement operations. Fortunately, the DEA is now permitted to travel outside the Kabul city limits, if specific security criteria can be met. This expanded travel will greatly increase our ability to conduct operations and gather intelligence. We also have increased our staffing levels in Afghanistan to more effectively complete our mission. . . .

The DEA has established the National Interdiction Unit (NIU), which is comprised of CNP-A officers who have been selected to work in narcotic enforcement operations with the Kabul CO. . . .

With DEA advisory assistance, training, and mentoring, we anticipate the NIU will be capable of conducting independent operations within two years. These officers also will be working with the DEA's newly initiated Foreign-deployed Advisory Support Team Agents. Since October 2004, 77 Counternarcotics Police-Afghanistan (CNP-A) NIU officers have graduated from their six-week training program and are operationally deployed. Included in this number are six female officers. The involvement of the female officers is of particular significance, due to cultural sensitivities, which prohibit women from being touched or searched by male law enforcement officers. These female officers will ensure that female suspects can be questioned, searched, and detained, if necessary. It is expected that, by April 2005, 100 NIU officers will have completed training and will work directly with the Kabul Country Office and other DEA entities.

Operation Containment was initiated in an attempt to place a security belt around Afghanistan, which would prevent processing chemicals from entering the country and opium and heroin from leaving.

Foreign-Deployed Advisory and Support Teams

In support of the "Five Pillar Plan," we have initiated the Foreign-deployed Advisory Support Teams (FAST). As early as March 30th, [2005,] the FAST groups may begin their initial deployment in Afghanistan. The FAST program directly improves the DEA's work force and capabilities in Afghanistan by enhancing connectivity with its Afghan counterparts to identify, target, investigate, disrupt or dismantle transnational drug trafficking operations in the region. The FAST groups will provide guidance to their Afghan counterparts, while conducting bilateral investigations aimed at the region's trafficking organizations. The FAST groups, which are supported and largely funded by the Department of Defense, also will help with the destruction of existing opium storage sites, clandestine heroin processing labs, and precursor chemical supplies. . . .

Operation Containment

DEA's participation in the Five Pillar Plan is an expansion of the DEA-led Operation Containment, which was initiated in 2002. The intensive, multi-national program known as Operation Containment was initiated in an attempt to place a security belt around Afghanistan, which would prevent processing chemicals from entering the country and opium and heroin from leaving. This program was necessary due to the lack of fully developed institutional systems for drug enforcement in Afghanistan, such as courts and law enforcement agencies. This program involves countries in Central Asia, the Caucasus, the Middle East, Europe, and Russia and has the participation of 19 countries. Through Operation Containment, in May 2003, the DEA was also able to establish a 25-member Sensitive Investigative Unit (SIU) in neighboring Uzbekistan—a country critical to containing the threat of Afghan opium entering Central Asia for further transit to Russia and Western Europe.

The success of this multi-national cooperative program has been tremendous. Prior to the initiation of Operation Containment, in 2002, only 407 kilograms [897 pounds] of heroin were seized. In FY [fiscal year] 2004, Operation Containment resulted in the seizure of 14.9 metric tons [16.4 tons] of heroin, 7.7 metric tons [8.4 tons] of morphine base, 5.9 metric tons [6.5 tons] of opium gum, approximately 3.27 metric tons [3.6 tons] of precursor chemicals, 77 metric tons

[84.8 tons] of cannabis, 11 heroin labs, and the arrest of 498 individuals, as well as the dismantlement or disruption of major distribution and transportation organizations involved in the Southwest Asian heroin drug trade. . . .

As of December 31, 2004, the DEA had identified 45 percent of the organizations on the Department of State's Foreign Terrorist Organizations list as having possible ties to the drug trade.

Drugs and Terrorism

In the past, terrorist groups derived much of their funding and support from state sponsors; however, with increased international pressure, many of these sources have become less reliable and, in some instances, disappeared altogether. As a result, terrorist groups have turned to alternative sources of financing, including fundraising from sympathizers and non-governmental organizations, as well as criminal activities, such as arms trafficking, money laundering, kidnap-for-ransom, extortion, racketeering, and drug trafficking. . . .

Although the DEA has evidence that some terrorist groups are involved in drug trafficking, the drug trade continues to be dominated at all levels by traditional drug trafficking organizations. The DEA does not specifically target terrorist groups, except those that are involved as major drug trafficking or money laundering organizations. For example, the DEA has achieved stunning successes in investigating, indicting, and causing the arrest of high-level narco-terrorists in Colombia that are on the Department of State's Foreign Terrorist Organizations list. Additionally, the DEA's intelligence program is working very closely with law enforcement and the Intelligence Community to identify and anticipate emerging threats posed by the links between drugs and terrorism.

As of December 31, 2004, the DEA had identified 45 percent (18 of 40) of the organizations on the Department of

State's Foreign Terrorist Organizations list as having possible ties to the drug trade. In addition, it is noteworthy as of February 18, 2005, 13 of the 42 organizations on the Department's Consolidated Priority Organization Target (CPOT) list—the "Most Wanted" drug trafficking and money laundering organizations believed to be primarily responsible for our nation's illicit drug supply—had links to these Foreign Terrorist Organizations.

The DEA continues to take an active leadership role in the multi-national efforts to combat the drug threat posed by Afghanistan. To date, our efforts have included increasing staffing levels in the Kabul Country Office and assigning our Assistant Administrator for Intelligence to lead the U.S. Embassy's Office of Drug Control Policy in Kabul. In addition, the FAST groups are nearing their initial deployment in Afghanistan, and we will continue working with our law enforcement partners in Operation Containment. We are confident that these efforts, and those of other U.S. Government agencies, Afghan law enforcement, and our other law enforcement partners, will lead to a reduction of opium production, and ultimately, the stabilization of Afghanistan and the region.

2

The U.S. Drug War in Afghanistan Undermines Antiterrorist Efforts

Ted Galen Carpenter

Ted Galen Carpenter is vice president for defense and foreign policy studies at the Cato Institute, a libertarian think tank. He is the author or editor of sixteen books on international affairs, including Bad Neighbor Policy: Washington's Futile War on Drugs in Latin America.

The money from opium and heroin production supports hundreds of thousands of people in Afghanistan and provides nearly half of that nation's gross domestic product. Despite the relative prosperity that heroin production provides to average Afghan families, the U.S. government is attempting to disrupt the trade, thereby condemning thousands to poverty. Unfortunately, those affected by the drug eradication programs are easily recruited by terrorist organizations. In addition, many powerful warlords make significant portions of their incomes from the heroin trade. These leaders, who have helped the United States fight the al Qaeda terrorist network, are now turning against the United States because of government efforts to disrupt opium production. If heroin was made legal in the West, prices would drop drastically, the narcotics trade would dry up, and terrorists

Ted Galen Carpenter, "How the Drug War in Afghanistan Undermines America's War on Terror," Cato.org, November 10, 2004. Reproduced by permission.

would be defunded. The United States must recognize this unfortunate reality and end its misguided drug war in Afghanistan.

The war on drugs is interfering with the U.S. effort to destroy Al Qaeda and the Taliban [the former Afghan ruling party] in Afghanistan. U.S. officials increasingly want to eradicate drugs as well as nurture Afghanistan's embryonic democracy, symbolized by the pro-Western regime of President Hamid Karzai. They need to face the reality that it is not possible to accomplish both objectives.

An especially troubling indicator came in August 2004 when Secretary of Defense Donald Rumsfeld stated that drug eradication in Afghanistan was a high priority of the [George W.] Bush administration and indicated that the United States and its coalition partners were in the process of formulating a "master plan" for dealing with the problem. "The danger a large drug trade poses in this country is too serious to ignore," Rumsfeld said. "The inevitable result is to corrupt the government and way of life, and that would be most unfortunate."

The secretary skirted the issue of what specific role U.S. troops would play in the intensified drug eradication effort. It soon became clear that U.S. military commanders in Afghanistan were less than thrilled at the prospect of becoming glorified narcotics cops. Less than a week after Rumsfeld's statement, Maj. Gen. Eric T. Olson, the commander of Combined Task Force 76 in Kandahar, stated bluntly that "at this point in time, U.S. troops will not be involved in counterdrug or counternarcotics operations at all."

"A Failure of Farcical Proportions"

Olson seemed to be out of step with his boss, but his comments reflect the long-standing reluctance of U.S. military personnel to complicate their mission of eradicating the remaining Al Qaeda and Taliban forces by becoming entangled in the complex issue of drug trafficking. Drug eradication "wasn't high on the list" admitted a Green Beret officer in 2003. "We pressured the warlords not to engage in the activity, but with all the opium in their caches, we knew . . . that they were not going to let it rot." The official U.S. military policy has been to destroy drug processing facilities (not crops) only if they are discovered "incidental to military operations and if the mission permits." German troops, operating in Afghanistan as part of a NATO [North Atlantic Treaty Organization] peacekeeping force, have adopted an even more laissez-faire attitude. They maintain a small garrison in the town of Kunduz, which lies in the middle of opium country, but the garrison's orders have been to refrain from interfering with the drug trade.

To the extent that the coalition forces in Afghanistan have pursued anti-drug initiatives at all, the United States has pushed its British partners to assume primary responsibility. The British effort, launched in 2002, consisted largely of offering Afghan farmers financial inducements to give up the cultivation of opium in favor of other crops. The strategy has not worked any better than it has in other parts of the world where it has been tried. Most farmers participating in the British program simply pocketed the money and continued to grow opium. Indeed, many of them seemed to regard the stipend as additional operating capital and actually expanded their production. One British critic described the effort as "a failure of farcical proportions." . . .

Pressure to Do Something

There are several reasons why Washington is now making the anti-drug campaign a high priority. Congressional pressure is mounting on the Bush administration to make counternarcotics goals a significant part of the U.S. military mission in Afghanistan. Influential members of Congress, such as Rep. Henry Hyde (R-IL), chairman of the House International

Relations Committee, have made it clear that they want action on the drug front. Although not specifically advocating crop eradication measures, Hyde has urged the Pentagon to treat all opium labs and storage areas in Afghanistan as "legitimate military targets and utilize narcotics-related intelligence to locate other such targets."

Another factor is that the United States is coming under increasing pressure from Afghanistan's neighbors in Central Asia and from drug-consuming nations in Europe to "do something" about the flood of narcotics coming out of that country. Russia has been especially outspoken. [In 2003], Gen. Viktor Cherkessov, the head of Russia's new drug enforcement agency, stated that drug production in Afghanistan had increased "catastrophically" and that the United States was not using its resources "to the fullest extent" to curtail production of Afghan opium. Russian president Vladimir Putin was considerably less diplomatic in criticizing U.S. and NATO forces in September 2004. "They're doing almost nothing, not even just to reduce the drugs problem," Putin fumed. "They should get more involved and not just watch as caravans [transporting opium] roam all over Afghanistan."

The Bush administration is sensitive to both congressional pressure and criticism from foreign capitals. The latter is especially true when it comes from an important ally in the war against radical Islamic terrorism. But other factors are even more important. Rumsfeld alluded to a critical reason for heightened U.S. concern—the potential for the drug commerce to corrupt Afghanistan's entire economic and political structure. Robert B. Charles, assistant secretary of state for international narcotics and law enforcement affairs, emphasized the same point:

> Stability in Afghanistan cannot be achieved without addressing the drug issue, and counternarcotics programs cannot be deferred to a later date. Afghanistan is already at risk of its narco-economy leading unintentionally but inexorably

to the evolution of a narco-state, with deeply entrenched public corruption and complicity in the drug trade undermining stability, containment of other threats, and all our assistance programs.

There are ample reasons for those concerns. Although arrests for narcotics trafficking are made from time to time, one police official admitted that "one thousand dollars gets you out of any trouble." Indeed, even some high level officials of the Karzai government (including the vice president who was assassinated last year) are reputed to have ties to the drug trade. . . .

U.S. officials are deeply concerned about the opium trade providing a lucrative source of revenue for the Taliban, Al Qaeda, and other enemies of the U.S.-backed . . . government.

Funding Terrorists

In addition to the general problem of corruption caused by drug money, U.S. officials are deeply concerned about the opium trade providing a lucrative source of revenue for the Taliban, Al Qaeda, and other enemies of the U.S.-backed Karzai government. Charles noted that the drug trade had helped the Taliban regime stay in power during the late 1990s. Indeed, the DEA [U.S. Drug Enforcement Administration] estimated that the Taliban collected more than $40 million a year in profits from the opium trade, with some of the cash going to terrorist groups that operated out of that country. Today, according to Charles, "there are strong indications that these heroin drug profits provide funds, to varying degrees, to Taliban remnants, al Qaeda, destabilizing regional warlords, and other terrorist and extremist elements in the region." Concerns about that factor were heightened [in 2003] when the U.S. Navy intercepted at least two drug shipments and detained merchant crews that included individuals directly linked to Al Qaeda.

There is little doubt that terrorist and other anti-government forces profit from the drug trade. What anti-drug crusaders refuse to acknowledge, however, is that the connection between drug trafficking and terrorism is a direct result of making drugs illegal. Not surprisingly, terrorist groups in Afghanistan and other countries are quick to exploit such a vast source of potential funding. Absent a worldwide prohibitionist policy, the profit margins in drug trafficking would be a tiny fraction of their current levels, and terrorist groups would have to seek other sources of revenue.

Since U.S. forces and their Northern Alliance allies overthrew the Taliban in late 2001, the drug commerce has been even more prominent.

In any case, the United States faces a serious dilemma if it conducts a vigorous drug eradication campaign in Afghanistan in an effort to dry up the funds flowing to Al Qaeda and the Taliban. Those are clearly not the only factions involved in drug trafficking. Many of Karzai's political allies are warlords who control the drug trade in their respective regions. Some of these individuals backed the Taliban when that faction was in power, switching sides only when the United States launched its military offensive in Afghanistan in October 2001. There is a serious risk that an anti-drug campaign might cause them to change their allegiance yet again. Even the pro-drug-war *Washington Times* conceded that "a number of heavily armed Tajik tribal leaders that have not been hostile to U.S. forces could lash out if their drug interests are directly and aggressively challenged." In addition to the need to placate cooperative warlords, the U.S.-led coalition relies on poppy growers to spy on movements of Taliban remnants and Al

Qaeda units. Disrupting the opium crop might alienate those crucial sources of information.

The Importance of the Drug Trade in Afghanistan

The drug trade is a central feature of Afghanistan's economy. That was not always the case, however. Before the Soviet invasion in 1979, Afghanistan was not a major factor in the drug trade. But the Soviet occupation and resulting insurgency by Islamic forces devastated the country's infrastructure, making it nearly impossible to continue the traditional forms of agriculture and other economic activities. . . .

In addition, various factions in the anti-Soviet Afghan resistance discovered that trafficking in drugs was a reliable and extensive source of revenue. Afghanistan gradually became one of the leading sources of opium poppies and, therefore, the heroin supply. Indeed, there has been a steady upward trend in opium production for more than two decades.

Very little has changed on the drug front following the end of the Soviet occupation. Violent political factionalism convulsed Afghanistan in the 1990s, gradually coalescing into a civil war between the radical Islamic Taliban regime in Kabul (dominated by the Pashtuns, the largest ethnic group in the country) and the predominantly Uzbek and Tajik Northern Alliance. Both sides were extensively involved in the drug trade to finance their war efforts.

The only significant interruption to the upward trend in drug commerce occurred in 2001 following an edict by the Taliban regime banning opium cultivation on pain of death. (Taliban leaders had an ulterior motive for that move. They had previously stockpiled large quantities of opium and wanted to create a temporary scarcity to drive up prices and fill the regime's coffers with additional revenue.) Since U.S. forces and their Northern Alliance allies overthrew the Taliban in late 2001, the drug commerce has been even more prominent. According to the United Nations Office on Drugs and Crime, the trade now amounts to approximately $2.3 billion—more than half as much as impoverished Afghanistan's legitimate annual gross domestic product. The International Monetary Fund calculates that the drug trade makes up at least 40 percent and perhaps as much as 60 percent of the country's entire GDP [gross domestic product].

For many . . . people, opium poppy crops and other aspects of drug commerce are the difference between modest prosperity and destitution.

The World's Supplier

Today, Afghanistan accounts for approximately 75 percent of the world's opium supply. Production is soaring. The country's poppy crop [in 2004] is set to break all records. CIA [Central Intelligence Agency] figures reportedly show cultivation approaching 250,000 acres, up more than 60 percent from the 2003 levels. The previous record was 160,000 acres in 2000. . . .

Some 264,000 families are estimated to be involved in growing opium poppies. Even measured on the basis of nuclear families, that translates into roughly 1.7 million people—about 6 percent of Afghanistan's population. Given the role of extended families and clans in Afghan society, the number of people affected is much greater than that. Indeed, it is likely that 20 to 30 percent of the population is involved directly or indirectly in the drug trade. For many of those people, opium poppy crops and other aspects of drug commerce are the difference between modest prosperity and destitution. They will not look kindly on efforts to destroy their livelihood.

That is especially true of the Pashtun farmers in southern and eastern Afghanistan, the core of Karzai's political constituency. As one Western diplomat in Afghanistan told Reuters news service: "If he bulldozes in and destroys crops, if he arrests and punishes farmers, they're definitely going to think that the Taliban have a point when they say the government is bad." ...

Crop Substitution Strategies Fail

The response of the United States and its coalition partners to this dilemma is to emphasize crop substitution programs as well as eradication of the opium crop. The idea is to bribe farmers into growing legal crops instead of poppies. Crop substitution is a strategy with a long and undistinguished pedigree. Since the mid-1980s, Washington has pursued a similar policy in the drug-source countries of South America. Virtually all of those programs have failed—most of them dismally.

Economic realities doom crop substitution schemes. Afghan farmers can typically make between 10 and 30 times as much growing opium poppies as they can any legal crop. The prohibitionist policy that the United States and other drug-consuming countries continue to pursue guarantees a huge black market premium for all illegal drugs. Drug traffickers can pay whatever price is necessary to get farmers to cultivate drug crops and still enjoy an enormous profit for their portion of the supply pipeline. Legal crops simply cannot compete financially.

The same problem undermines more ambitious economic development schemes to give drug crop farmers nonagricultural alternatives. Indeed, the South American experience indicates that such programs often simply provide additional capital and other benefits to those who have no intention of abandoning the drug trade. For example, aid monies to improve the transportation infrastructure in recipient countries by building modern roads into remote areas (an effort now under way in Afghanistan as well) make it easier for drug farmers to get their crops to market and may open new areas to drug cultivation.

Misguided U.S. Policies

Despite those daunting economic realities, the U.S. government is putting increased pressure on the fragile Karzai government to crack down on drug crop cultivation. And the Afghan regime is responding. In late September 2004, Afghan police and security forces destroyed 47 laboratories used to refine heroin from opium and seized 61 tons of narcotics in a series of raids near the border with Pakistan. (Although the seizure sounds impressive, Afghanistan produced more than 3,600 tons of opium [in 2003].)

U.S. pressure on the Karzai government is a big mistake. The Taliban and their Al Qaeda allies are resurgent in Afghanistan, especially in the southern part of the country. If zealous American drug warriors alienate hundreds of thousands of Afghan farmers, the Karzai government's hold on power, which is none too secure now, could become even more precarious. Washington would then face the unpalatable choice of letting radical Islamists regain power or sending more U.S. troops to suppress the insurgency.

The drug war is a dangerous distraction in the campaign to destroy [the Taliban and al Qaeda].

U.S. officials need to keep their priorities straight. Our mortal enemy is Al Qaeda and the Taliban regime that made Afghanistan into a sanctuary for that terrorist organization. The drug war is a dangerous distraction in the campaign to destroy those forces. Recognizing that security considerations sometimes trump other objectives would hardly be an unprecedented move by Washington. U.S. agencies quietly ignored the drug-trafficking activities of anti-communist factions in Central America during the 1980s when the primary goal was to keep those countries out of the Soviet orbit. In the early 1990s, the United States also eased its pressure on Peru's government regarding the drug eradication issue when President Alberto Fujimori concluded that a higher priority had to be given to winning coca farmers away from the Maoist Shining Path guerrilla movement.

U.S. officials should adopt a similar pragmatic policy in Afghanistan and look the other way regarding the drug-trafficking activities of friendly warlords. And above all, the U.S. military must not become the enemy of Afghan farmers whose livelihood depends on opium poppy cultivation. True, some of the funds from the drug trade will find their way into the coffers of the Taliban and Al Qaeda. That is an inevitable side effect of a global prohibitionist policy that creates such an enormous profit from illegal drugs. But alienating pro-Western Afghan factions in an effort to disrupt the flow of revenue to the Islamic radicals is too high a price to pay. Washington should stop putting pressure on the Afghan government to pursue crop eradication programs and undermine the economic well-being of its own population. U.S. leaders also should refrain from trying to make U.S. soldiers into anti-drug crusaders: they have a difficult enough job fighting their terrorist adversaries in Afghanistan. Even those policymakers who oppose ending the war on drugs as a general matter ought to recognize that, in this case, the war against radical Islamic terrorism must take priority.

3

Heroin Is an Addictive and Dangerous Drug

National Institute on Drug Abuse

The National Institute on Drug Abuse conducts research into scientific methods that may be used to cure drug addiction.

Heroin abuse results in addiction, sickness, and death. Use of the drug is a serious problem, as shown by the increasing number of heroin-related emergency room visits and deaths from overdoses. People who take heroin are likely to find themselves physically addicted and unable to quit. Although a relatively small number of teenagers experiment with the drug, the consequences of heroin abuse are so negative that the use of this drug must be curtailed.

Heroin is an addictive drug, and its use is a serious problem in America. Recent studies suggest a shift from injecting heroin to snorting or smoking because of increased purity and the misconception that these forms are safer.

Heroin is processed from morphine, a naturally occurring substance extracted from the seedpod of the Asian poppy plant. Heroin usually appears as a white or brown powder. Street names for heroin include "smack," "H," "skag," and "junk." Other names may refer to types of heroin produced in a specific geographical area, such as "Mexican black tar."

National Institute on Drug Abuse, "NIDA InfoFacts: Heroin," March 2005. www.nida.nih.gov/Infofacts/heroin.html.

Health Hazards

Heroin abuse is associated with serious health conditions, including fatal overdose, spontaneous abortion, collapsed veins, and, particularly in users who inject the drug, infectious diseases, including HIV/AIDS and hepatitis.

Street heroin may have additives that do not readily dissolve and result in clogging the blood vessels that lead to the lungs, liver, kidneys, or brain.

The short-term effects of heroin abuse appear soon after a single dose and disappear in a few hours. After an injection of heroin, the user reports feeling a surge of euphoria ("rush") accompanied by a warm flushing of the skin, a dry mouth, and heavy extremities. Following this initial euphoria, the user goes "on the nod," an alternately wakeful and drowsy state. Mental functioning becomes clouded due to the depression of the central nervous system. Long-term effects of heroin appear after repeated use for some period of time. Chronic users may develop collapsed veins, infection of the heart lining and valves, abscesses, cellulitis, and liver disease. Pulmonary complications, including various types of pneumonia, may result from the poor health condition of the abuser, as well as from heroin's depressing effects on respiration.

Heroin abuse during pregnancy and its many associated environmental factors (e.g., lack of prenatal care) have been associated with adverse consequences, including low birth weight, an important risk factor for later developmental delay.

In addition to the effects of the drug itself, street heroin may have additives that do not readily dissolve and result in clogging the blood vessels that lead to the lungs, liver, kidneys, or brain. This can cause infection or even death of small patches of cells in vital organs.

The Drug Abuse Warning Network lists heroin/morphine among the four most frequently mentioned drugs reported in drug-related death cases in 2002. Nationwide, heroin emergency department mentions were statistically unchanged from 2001 to 2002, but have increased 35 percent since 1995.

Sudden withdrawal by heavily dependent users who are in poor health is occasionally fatal.

Tolerance, Addiction, and Withdrawal

With regular heroin use, tolerance develops. This means the abuser must use more heroin to achieve the same intensity of effect. As higher doses are used over time, physical dependence and addiction develop. With physical dependence, the body has adapted to the presence of the drug and withdrawal symptoms may occur if use is reduced or stopped.

Withdrawal, which in regular abusers may occur as early as a few hours after the last administration, produces drug craving, restlessness, muscle and bone pain, insomnia, diarrhea and vomiting, cold flashes with goose bumps ("cold turkey"), kicking movements ("kicking the habit"), and other symptoms. Major withdrawal symptoms peak between 48 and 72 hours after the last dose and subside after about a week. Sudden withdrawal by heavily dependent users who are in poor health is occasionally fatal, although heroin withdrawal is considered less dangerous than alcohol or barbiturate withdrawal.

Treatment

There is a broad range of treatment options for heroin addiction, including medications as well as behavioral therapies. Science has taught us that when medication treatment is integrated with other supportive services, patients are often able to stop heroin . . . use and return to more stable and productive lives.

In November 1997, the National Institutes of Health (NIH) convened a Consensus Panel on Effective Medical Treatment of Heroin Addiction. The panel of national experts concluded that opiate drug addictions are diseases of the brain and medical disorders that indeed can be treated effectively. The panel strongly recommended (1) broader access to methadone maintenance treatment programs for people who are addicted to heroin or other opiate drugs; and (2) the Federal and State regulations and other barriers impeding this access be eliminated. This panel also stressed the importance of providing substance abuse counseling, psychosocial therapies, and other supportive services to enhance retention and successful outcomes in methadone maintenance treatment programs. . . .

Methadone, a synthetic opiate medication that blocks the effects of heroin for about 24 hours, has a proven record of success when prescribed at a high enough dosage level for people addicted to heroin. Other approved medications are naloxone, which is used to treat cases of overdose, and naltrexone, both of which block the effects of morphine, heroin, and other opiates.

For the pregnant heroin abuser, methadone maintenance combined with prenatal care and a comprehensive drug treatment program can improve many of the detrimental maternal and neonatal outcomes associated with untreated heroin abuse. There is preliminary evidence that buprenorphine also is safe and effective in treating heroin dependence during pregnancy, although infants exposed to methadone or buprenorphine during pregnancy typically require treatment for withdrawal symptoms. For women who do not want or are not able to receive pharmacotherapy for their heroin addiction, detoxification from opiates during pregnancy can be accomplished with relative safety, although the likelihood of relapse to heroin use should be considered.

Buprenorphine is a recent addition to the array of medications now available for treating addiction to heroin and other opiates. This medication is different from methadone in that it offers less risk of addiction and can be dispensed in the privacy of a doctor's office. Several other medications for use in heroin treatment programs are also under study.

There are many effective behavioral treatments available for heroin addiction. These can include residential and outpatient approaches. Several new behavioral therapies are showing particular promise for heroin addiction. Contingency management therapy uses a voucher-based system, where patients earn "points" based on negative drug tests, which they can exchange for items that encourage healthful living. Cognitive-behavioral interventions are designed to help modify the patient's thinking, expectancies, and behaviors and to increase skills in coping with various life stressors.

A Growing Concern

In December 2003, CEWG [Community Epidemiology Work Group] members reported that heroin indicators were mixed but relatively stable, continuing at higher levels in Northeastern, north-central, and mid-Atlantic areas where high-purity powder is available, and also in the Northwest where black tar heroin predominates. Heroin injection and the health risks associated with it, such as the spread of HIV/AIDS and hepatitis C, are of growing concern at several CEWG sites. In 2002, rates of heroin emergency department mentions exceeded 200 per 100,000 in Chicago, Newark, and Baltimore and exceeded 100 per 100,000 in Seattle, New York City, San Francisco, Boston, and Philadelphia. The reporting of heroin/opiate-related deaths was highest in Detroit (464) and Philadelphia (111)

National Survey on Drug Use and Health

The 2003 [National Survey on Drug Use and Health] reports stability at low levels for heroin use among young people. In 2002, 13,000 youth between the ages of 12 and 17 had used heroin at least once in the past year ("annual" use), compared with 12,000 in 2003. Among the general population age 12 and older, 404,000 had used annually in 2002, compared with 314,000 in 2003.

4

The Addictive Powers of Heroin Are Exaggerated

Jacob Sullum

Jacob Sullum is a senior editor of Reason, *a libertarian political journal.*

Heroin is portrayed by antidrug crusaders as the world's most dangerous, addictive drug. People are told that only one dose of heroin will lead to a lifetime of addiction. Those who spread this message ignore the fact that out of 3 to 4 million heroin users in the United States, only about 10 percent are daily users. By comparison, about 15 percent of drinkers are alcoholics, and one-third of cigarette smokers have found that they cannot quit for even one day. Most heroin addicts, however, either limit their intake to once or twice a month or quit taking the drug altogether for extended periods of time. By portraying heroin as the ultimate evil, prohibitionists have given the drug an allure that it does not deserve.

In 1992 *The New York Times* carried a front page story about a successful businessman who happened to be a regular heroin user. It began: "He is an executive in a company in New York, lives in a condo on the Upper East Side of Manhattan, drives an expensive car, plays tennis in the Hamptons and vacations with his wife in Europe and the Caribbean. But unknown to office colleagues, friends, and most of his family, the man is also a longtime heroin user. He says he finds heroin relaxing and pleasurable and has seen no reason to stop using it until the woman he recently married insisted that he do so. 'The drug is an enhancement of my life', he said. 'I see it as similar to a guy coming home and having a drink of alcohol. Only alcohol has never done it for me.'"

The *Times* noted that "nearly everything about the 44-year-old executive . . . seems to fly in the face of widely held perceptions about heroin users." The reporter who wrote the story and his editors seemed uncomfortable with contradicting official anti-drug propaganda, which depicts heroin use as incompatible with a satisfying, productive life. The headline read, "Executive's Secret Struggle with Heroin's Powerful Grip," which sounds more like a cautionary tale than a success story. And the *Times* hastened to add that heroin users "are flirting with disaster." It conceded that "heroin does not damage the organs as, for instance, heavy alcohol use does." But it cited the risk of arrest, overdose, AIDS, and hepatitis—without noting that all of these risks are created or exacerbated by prohibition.

The idea that a drug can compel the person who consumes it to continue consuming it is one of the most important beliefs underlying the war on drugs.

The general thrust of the piece was: Here is a privileged man who is tempting fate by messing around with a very dangerous drug. He may have escaped disaster so far, but unless he quits he will probably end up dead or in prison.

That is not the way the businessman saw his situation. He said he had decided to give up heroin only because his wife did not approve of the habit. "In my heart," he said, "I really don't feel there's anything wrong with using heroin. But there doesn't seem to be any way in the world I can persuade my wife to grant me this space in our relationship. I don't want to lose her, so I'm making this effort."

A Long Tradition of Anti-Drug Propaganda

Judging from the "widely held perceptions about heroin users" mentioned by the *Times*, that effort was bound to fail. The conventional view of heroin, which powerfully shapes the popular understanding of addiction, is nicely summed up in the journalist Martin Booth's 1996 history of opium. "Addiction is the compulsive taking of drugs which have such a hold over the addict he or she cannot stop using them without suffering severe symptoms and even death," he writes. "Opiate dependence . . . is as fundamental to an addict's existence as food and water, a physio-chemical fact: an addict's body is chemically reliant upon its drug for opiates actually alter the body's chemistry so it cannot function properly without being periodically primed. A hunger for the drug forms when the quantity in the bloodstream falls below a certain level. . . . Fail to feed the body and it deteriorates and may die from drug starvation." Booth also declares that "everyone . . . is a potential addict"; that "addiction can start with the very first dose"; and that "with continued use addiction is a certainty."

Booth's description is wrong or grossly misleading in every particular. To understand why is to recognize the fallacies underlying a reductionist, drug-centered view of addiction in which chemicals force themselves on people—a view that skeptics such as the maverick psychiatrist Thomas Szasz and the psychologist Stanton Peele have long questioned. The idea that a drug can compel the person who consumes it to continue consuming it is one of the most important beliefs underlying the war on drugs, because this power makes possible all the other evils to which drug use supposedly leads.

When Martin Booth tells us that anyone can be addicted to heroin, that it may take just one dose, and that it will certainly happen to you if you're foolish enough to repeat the experiment, he is drawing on a long tradition of anti-drug propaganda. As the sociologist Harry G. Levine has shown, the original model for such warnings was not heroin or opium but alcohol. "The idea that drugs are inherently addicting," Levine wrote in 1978, "was first systematically worked out for alcohol and then extended to other substances. Long before opium was popularly accepted as addicting, alcohol was so regarded." The dry [anti-alcohol] crusaders 'of the 19th and early 20th centuries taught that every tippler was a potential drunkard, that a glass of beer was the first step on the road to ruin, and that repeated use of distilled spirits made addiction virtually inevitable. Today, when a kitchen wrecked by a skinny model wielding a frying pan [in an anti-drug TV commercial] is supposed to symbolize the havoc caused by a snort of heroin, similar assumptions about opiates are even more widely held, and they likewise are based more on faith than facts.

Heroin users commonly drift in and out of their habits, going through periods of abstinence and returning to the drug long after any physical discomfort has faded away.

Withdrawal Penalty

Beginning early in the 20th century, Stanton Peele notes, heroin "came to be seen in American society as the nonpareil drug of addiction—as leading inescapably from even the most casual contact to an intractable dependence, withdrawal from which was traumatic and unthinkable for the addict." According to this view, reflected in Booth's gloss and other popular portrayals, the potentially fatal agony of withdrawal is the gun that heroin holds to the addict's head. These accounts greatly exaggerate both the severity and the importance of withdrawal symptoms.

Heroin addicts who abruptly stop using the drug commonly report flu-like symptoms, which may include chills, sweating, runny nose and eyes, muscular aches, stomach cramps, nausea, diarrhea, or headaches. While certainly unpleasant, the experience is not life threatening. Indeed, addicts who have developed tolerance (needing higher doses to achieve the same effect) often voluntarily undergo withdrawal so they can begin using heroin again at a lower dose, thereby reducing the cost of their habit. Another sign that fear of withdrawal symptoms is not the essence of addiction is the fact that heroin users commonly drift in and out of their habits, going through periods of abstinence and returning to the drug long after any physical discomfort has faded away. Indeed, the observation that detoxification is not tantamount to overcoming an addiction, that addicts typically will try repeatedly before successfully kicking the habit, is a commonplace of drug treatment.

More evidence that withdrawal has been overemphasized as a motivation for using opiates comes from patients who take narcotic painkillers over extended periods of time. Like heroin addicts, they develop "physical dependence" and experience withdrawal symptoms when they stop taking the drugs. But studies conducted during the last two decades have consistently found that patients in pain who receive opioids (opiates or synthetics with similar effects) rarely become addicted.

Pain experts emphasize that physical dependence should not be confused with addiction, which requires a psychological component: a persistent desire to use the substance for its mood-altering effects. Critics have long complained that unreasonable fears about narcotic addiction discourage adequate pain treatment. In 1989 Charles Schuster, then director of the National Institute on Drug Abuse, confessed, "We have been so effective in warning the medical establishment and the public in general about the inappropriate use of opi-

ates that we have endowed these drugs with a mysterious power to enslave that is overrated."

Although popular perceptions lag behind, the point made by pain specialists—that "physical dependence" is not the same as addiction—is now widely accepted by professionals who deal with drug problems. But under the heroin-based model that prevailed until the 1970s, tolerance and withdrawal symptoms were considered the hallmarks of addiction. By this standard, drugs such as nicotine and cocaine were not truly addictive; they were merely "habituating." That distinction proved untenable, given the difficulty that people often had in giving up substances that were not considered addictive.

Having hijacked the term addiction, which in its original sense referred to any strong habit, psychiatrists ultimately abandoned it in favor of substance dependence. . . . In addition to tolerance and withdrawal, these include using more of the drug than intended; trying unsuccessfully to cut back; spending a lot of time getting the drug, using it, or recovering from its effects; giving up or reducing important social, occupational, or recreational activities because of drug use; and continuing use even while recognizing drug-related psychological or physical problems.

One can quibble with these criteria, especially since they are meant to be applied not by the drug user himself but by a government-licensed expert with whose judgment he may disagree. The possibility of such a conflict is all the more troubling because the evaluation may be involuntary (the result of an arrest, for example) and may have implications for the drug user's freedom. More fundamentally, classifying substance dependence as a "mental disorder" to be treated by medical doctors suggests that drug abuse is a disease, something that happens to people rather than something that people do. Yet it is clear from the description that we are talking about a pattern of behavior. Addiction is not simply a matter of introducing a chemical into someone's body, even if

it is done often enough to create tolerance and withdrawal symptoms. Conversely, someone who takes a steady dose of a drug and who can stop using it without physical distress may still be addicted to it.

Of all active heroin users . . . a large majority are not addicts: they are not physically or socially dysfunctional; they are not daily users and they do not seem to require treatment.

Simply Irresistible?

Even if addiction is not a physical compulsion, perhaps some drug experiences are so alluring that people find it impossible to resist them. Certainly that is heroin's reputation encapsulated in the title of a 1972 book: *It's So Good, Don't Even Try It Once.*

The fact that heroin use is so rare—involving, according to the government's data, something like 0.2 percent of the U.S. population in 2001—suggests that its appeal is much more limited than we've been led to believe. If heroin really is "so good," why does it have such a tiny share of the illegal drug market? Marijuana is more than 45 times as popular. The National Household Survey on Drug Abuse indicates that about 3 million Americans have used heroin in their lifetimes; of them, 15 percent had used it in the last year, 4 percent in the last month. These numbers suggest that the vast majority of heroin users either never become addicted or, if they do, manage to give the drug up. A survey of high school seniors found that 1 percent had used heroin in the previous year, while 0.1 percent had used it on 20 or more days in the previous month. Assuming that daily use is a reasonable proxy for opiate addiction, one in 10 of the students who had taken heroin in the last year might have qualified as addicts. These are not the sort of numbers you'd expect for a drug that's irresistible.

True, these surveys exclude certain groups in which heroin use is more common and in which a larger percentage of users probably could be described as addicts. The household survey misses people living on the street, in prisons, and in residential drug treatment programs, while the high school survey leaves out truants and dropouts. But even for the entire population of heroin users, the estimated addiction rates do not come close to matching heroin's reputation. A 1976 study by the drug researchers Leon G. Hunt and Carl D. Chambers estimated there were 3 or 4 million heroin users in the United States, perhaps 10 percent of them addicts. "Of all active heroin users," Hunt and Chambers wrote, "a large majority are not addicts: they are not physically or socially dysfunctional; they are not daily users and they do not seem to require treatment." A 1994 study based on data from the National Comorbidity Survey estimated that 23 percent of heroin users ever experience substance dependence.

The comparable rate for alcohol in that study was 15 percent, which seems to support the idea that heroin is more addictive: A larger percentage of the people who try it become heavy users, even though it's harder to get. At the same time, the fact that using heroin is illegal, expensive, risky, inconvenient, and almost universally condemned means that the people who nevertheless choose to do it repeatedly will tend to differ from people who choose to drink. They will be especially attracted to heroin's effects, the associated lifestyle, or both. In other words, heroin users are a self-selected group, less representative of the general population than alcohol users are, and they may be more inclined from the outset to form strong attachments to the drug.

The same study found that 32 percent of tobacco users had experienced substance dependence. Figures like that one are the basis for the claim that nicotine is "more addictive than heroin." After all, cigarette smokers typically go through a pack or so a day, so they're under the influence of nicotine every waking moment. Heroin users typically do not use their drug even once a day. Smokers offended by this comparison are quick to point out that they function fine, meeting their responsibilities at work and home despite their habit. This, they assume, is impossible for heroin users. Examples like the businessman described by *The New York Times* indicate otherwise. . . .

Without prohibition . . . a daily heroin habit would be far less burdensome and hazardous.

The Needle and the Damage Done

To a large extent, regular heroin use also can be separated from the terrible consequences that have come to be associated with it. Because of prohibition, users face the risk of arrest and imprisonment, the handicap of a criminal record, and the violence associated with the black market. The artificially high price of heroin, perhaps 40 or 50 times what it would otherwise cost, may lead to heavy debts, housing problems, poor nutrition, and theft. The inflated cost also encourages users to inject the drug, a more efficient but riskier mode of administration. The legal treatment of injection equipment, including restrictions on distribution and penalties for possession, encourages needle sharing, which spreads diseases such as AIDS and hepatitis. The unreliable quality and unpredictable purity associated with the black market can lead to poisoning and accidental overdoses.

Without prohibition, then, a daily heroin habit would be far less burdensome and hazardous. Heroin itself is much less likely to kill a user than the reckless combination of heroin with other depressants, such as alcohol or barbiturates. The federal government's Drug Abuse Warning Network counted 4,820 mentions of heroin or morphine (which are indistinguishable in the blood) by medical examiners in 1999. Only

438 of these deaths (9 percent) were listed as directly caused by an overdose of the opiate. Three-quarters of the deaths were caused by heroin/morphine in combination with other drugs. Provided the user avoids such mixtures, has access to a supply of reliable purity, and follows sanitary injection procedures, the health risks of long-term opiate consumption are minimal.

Only a very small share of the population ever uses [heroin], and a large majority of those who do never become addicted.

The comparison between heroin and nicotine is also instructive when it comes to the role of drug treatment. Although many smokers have a hard time quitting, those who succeed generally do so on their own. Surprisingly, the same may be true of heroin addicts. In the early 1960s, based on records kept by the Federal Bureau of Narcotics, sociologist Charles Winick concluded that narcotic addicts tend to "mature out" of the habit in their 30s. He suggested that "addiction may be a self-limiting process for perhaps two-thirds of addicts." Subsequent researchers have questioned Winick's assumptions, and other studies have come up with lower estimates. But it's clear that "natural recovery" is much more common than the public has been led to believe.

In a 1974 study of Vietnam veterans, only 12 percent of those who were addicted to heroin in Vietnam took up the habit again during the three years after their return to the United States. (This was not because they couldn't find heroin; half of them used it at least once after their return, generally without becoming addicted again.) Those who had undergone treatment (half of the group) were just as likely to be re-addicted as those who had not. Since those with stronger addictions were more likely to receive treatment, this does not necessarily mean that treatment was useless, but it clearly was not a prerequisite for giving up heroin.

Despite its reputation, then, heroin is neither irresistible nor inescapable. Only a very small share of the population ever uses it, and a large majority of those who do never become addicted. Even within the minority who develop a daily habit, most manage to stop using heroin, often without professional intervention. Yet heroin is still perceived as the paradigmatic voodoo drug, ineluctably turning its users into zombies who must obey its commands.

5

Media Glamorization of Heroin Influences Young People

Micheline Duterte, Kristin Hemphill, Terrence Murphy, and Sheigla Murphy

Micheline Duterte is a research associate at the Institute for Scientific Analysis and has worked on four National Institute on Drug Abuse (NIDA) studies involving ecstasy distribution, young heroin users, needle-exchange programs, drug use, and health care. Kristin Hemphill is a research associate at the Institute for Scientific Analysis (ISA) on studies of young heroin users and needle-exchange programs. Terrence Murphy, a lawyer, has worked as project director on three NIDA grants at ISA. Sheigla Murphy, a medical sociologist, is director of the Center of Substance Abuse Studies at the ISA.

For the past several decades, heroin use has been romanticized in books, films, magazines, and songs. This glamorization, dubbed "heroin chic," has influenced a new generation of addicts who cite the work of talented, rebellious, and often tragic junkies in order to justify their own addiction. For example, heroin-using rock stars have been extremely influential upon the behavior of addicts, as have certain fashion trends showcasing glassy-eyed

Micheline Duterte, Kristin Hemphill, Terrence Murphy, and Sheigla Murphy, "Tragic Beauties: Heroin Images and Heroin Users," *Contemporary Drug Problems*, Fall 2003. © 2003 by Federal Legal Publications, Inc. Reproduced by permission.

models with blank expressions. While many users are attracted to heroin for a variety of reasons, there is little doubt that the media play a role in influencing the lifestyles and behavior of addicts.

The continued popularity of "heroin chic," tattoos and body piercing among America's young adults reflects messages to and from a "rebel" youth culture. Into the new millennium, young people can be labeled the "post-AIDS" generation because they grew up living with the threat of HIV infection. The 1990s media coverage of HIV/AIDS ran concurrently with media representations that glamorized heroin, a drug often associated with HIV infection resulting from unsafe injection practices. The juxtaposition of media messages concerning disease on the one hand and fashionable heroin use on the other shaped youthful perceptions of heroin in ways that differ from the perceptions of past generations. Little research exists on the 18- to 25-year-old drug-using cohort's perceptions of heroin. In this [viewpoint], we explore the effects of media representations and youth culture identification on heroin initiation and continuation. The [phrase] "tragic beauties" is taken from an interview with one young heroin user; it is a fitting depiction of many other participants' fatalistic and sometimes romanticized attitudes toward heroin use and its consequences. More than merely a fashionable appearance, the concept of "tragic beauties" conveys young heroin users' notions of living artistic, rebellious lifestyles.

The media must be viewed as reflecting young people's heroin perceptions while also influencing them.

One outcome of the rise in heroin's visibility in popular culture is that heroin is regarded as "chic" in certain social milieus. [According to one 1999 study,] media portrayals that legitimize or even exalt illicit drug use may have a strong impact on youths' perceptions and acceptance of this behavior. News stories about actors, musicians, and other celebrities' heroin-related deaths or arrests have become commonplace. Films like *Drug Store Cowboy* (1988), *Pulp Fiction* (1994), *The Basketball Diaries* (1995), *Trainspotting* (1996), *High Art* (1997) and the [more] recent *Requiem for a Dream* (2001) focused on heroin users' all-consuming addiction to the point of life degradation. The characters in these movies are intriguing nonconformists living with the burden of heroin use, the quintessential "tragic beauties." Furthermore, heroin has long been associated with popular music. From [pioneering jazz musician] Charlie Parker to [grunge rock star] Kurt Cobain, heroin has been closely connected to the lives and deaths of numerous notable musicians. Some fans may want to experience a taste of these celebrities' exciting lifestyles; but are these media representations powerful enough to instigate young adults' heroin use? . . . In the analysis presented in this [viewpoint], we [argue] that the media must be viewed as reflecting young people's heroin perceptions while also influencing them.

Heroin, historically a taboo drug, is once again achieving a trendy status in some social circles. This phenomenon is related in part to the tendency to glamorize the "outsider". There are many youth groups and subcultures that idealize what goes against the mainstream, particularly if it reflects their perceptions of their own identity. . . .

Additionally, the media as a key element of commercial culture play a role in shaping the creation of subcultures, or "taste cultures," within our society. Youths form subcultures from shared interests in music (e.g., punks), art (e.g., graffiti artists), literature (e.g., Beatniks), hobbies (e.g., skaters) and moral beliefs (e.g., straights). The term "subcultural capital," [is used] to describe those things, both embodied and objectified, that represent individuals' absolute membership in particular subcultures, and heroin use may function as subcultural capital within some youth cultures. . . .

A Study of Young Heroin Users

We present selected preliminary findings from a National Institute on Drug Abuse-funded study titled "A Study of Young Heroin Users." Two white women, one Korean woman, one Filipina and one Latino (ranging in age from 21 to 26) conducted the interviews with heroin-using individuals. Each participant was screened to assess eligibility for the study and then was administered one in-depth life history interview and a structured questionnaire. Using both qualitative and quantitative data collection strategies, we investigated the heroin-using lifestyles of 102 young adult heroin users. The major areas of interest included, but were not limited to, (1) processes of initiation into heroin use, (2) factors influencing progressive heroin use, (3) reasons for utilizing specific routes of administration and changing routes of administration, (4) the ways in which young heroin users managed their everyday lives, (5) study participants' involvement in criminal activities and methods of procuring heroin, (6) perceptions of and attitudes toward drug-related health risks and harm-reduction practices, (7) and the impact of social networks on heroin initiation and continued use. . . . In order to be enrolled in the study, participants had to have used heroin five or more times within the 30 days preceeding the interview.

The study sample consisted of 102 young adults, 18–25 years old. There were 62 males and 40 females. An ethnic breakdown of the sample reveals that the vast majority of these young heroin users were white. There were seven Latino/a participants, six African-Americans, one Asian/Pacific Islander, one Native American, and two participants of mixed ethnicity. By reviewing the demographic characteristics of the clients of various treatment and health care agencies in San Francisco, we found that white males predominated in mentions of heroin-related problems. Therefore our sample closely mirrors the San Francisco heroin-using community for this age cohort.

Institutionalization during childhood and adolescence was common in our sample. Forty-five percent of the sample were institutionalized overall, with 19% having been in one institution during their childhood or adolescence, 14% in two, 10% in three, and 2% in four institutions. Early institutionalization included commitment prior to 18 years of age to drug treatment, Youth Authority, juvenile correctional facilities, foster care group homes, halfway homes, and mental institutions. Most participants who had been institutionalized were sent to drug treatment (63%). Clearly, drug treatment was not ultimately effective for these interviewees, since they were using heroin and other drugs at the time of interview.

Heroin experiences varied, but one recurring theme emerged: [addicts'] fascination with celebrities', rock musicians' and writers' heroin use.

Most of the participants grow up in unstable families, and the majority had left home during their adolescence. In fact, 64% were without permanent housing during the year before the interview. Many of them had some form of legal employment in the year preceding the interview (43%), but a majority of the interviewees panhandled (54%) or engaged in one or more illegal activities, like selling drugs and/or shoplifting, for income (62%). Relative to past studies of heroin users, these participants engaged in low levels of crime, rarely resorting to burglary or violent crimes to procure their heroin. Some participants lived on the streets or occupied an abandoned building ("squatted") with either a romantic partner (21%) or a close-knit group of friends (40%), sometimes referred to as a "street family."

After completing several of these interviews, it became evident that mass media portrayals of heroin were important to our participants. We analyzed the data to characterize the role of such media messages. We coded interview passages describing heroin images in the media, movies with heroin users, literature about heroin, and celebrities who used or died heroin-related deaths. Although this topic was not a focus of the original study design, it emerged as a salient theme when interviewees related their stories about their initial interest in and experimentation with heroin. . . .

Fascination with Heroin Use

Our study participants disclosed various reasons for their attraction to heroin. Heroin experiences varied, but one recurring theme emerged: their fascination with celebrities', rock musicians' and writers' heroin use. While most adamantly indicated that such influences were not isolated, comments concerning heroin depictions in the media were common. Some participants had little or no exposure to information about heroin use or heroin users through other sources. Interviewees' early drug education (e.g., D.A.R.E., Just Say No) in the 1980s and 1990s rarely addressed heroin use. Most often, the media were their primary source of information.

Our sample identified themselves as members of specific subcultures or social worlds, such as "gutter punk," "hippie," "industrial" and "goth." These distinct groups often desire to live on the fringes of society and to express themselves through their nonconformist lifestyles. In describing these groups' emotional metaphors, [researcher A.] Porter points out, "Punk represents rebellion, Industrial represents anger, Goth represents sadness." Particular media images can reflect and inspire the practices of these subcultures, especially when celebrities who have pioneered such social worlds are profiled. Drug use, or in this case heroin use, can be an element of such a subculture. Some of our study participants described their heroin initiation and continuation in terms of their subcultural identities.

Some perceived heroin as a drug used for artistic performance enhancement.

One interviewee, Craig [all names of interviewees are pseudonyms], grew up in a small town. Before the age of 16, he had minimal exposure to heroin users or heroin-using lifestyles. His conservative parents did not feel it was necessary to discuss drug use with their children. As a result, Craig had very little information about heroin except what he learned from friends who were already regular users. When he was 16, a heroin-using girlfriend introduced him to heroin. When we interviewed Craig at 22, we asked about his perceptions of heroin before his own use. He claimed to have had very little prior knowledge.

> Actually, I didn't know too much about it. You know, I mean, there's always all these anti-drug campaigns. So, I heard, you know, everyone's heard about drugs through those campaigns, but, I didn't know too much about it, you know. So I tried it. And it was like, uh, kind of a subculture that goes along with it. Those two girls who used were definitely a part of that. You know, [pioneering rock band] Velvet Underground, you know, they kinda idolized certain, you know, heroin addicts . . . mostly it was the music, you know, 70's subculture.

Craig raised a pertinent point when he associated his friends' heroin use with a particular music subculture. Music groups like the Velvet Underground generated a following within the punk subculture (some study participants identified themselves as punks). Such bands did not hide their heroin use or their feelings about the drug, often conspicuously spotlighting their heroin use with songs like Velvet Underground's "Heroin." Some interviewees cited their favorite musicians' heroin use as an added appeal of the drug. Participants also may have felt that they gained more of an insider knowledge of their subculture with heroin use—it may have become subcultural capital.

The Punk Rock Drug

One participant, a 21-year-old white male injector, recalled his perceptions of heroin prior to initiation. He first used at the age of 16 by "chasing the dragon" (inhaling smoke by burning the powder on aluminum foil) with China White, and eventually moved on to snorting and injecting heroin. When asked what he thought of heroin before he started using it, he described a relationship between heroin and his own decision to initiate heroin use.

> Okay, I was kinda like into punk rock and stuff. I mean, I guess I'd be called a punk rocker back then. And uh, that's like always, you know, it seems like the big punk rock drug or somethin'. And uh, you know, like, everybody, all my favorite musicians were ex-addicts, 'cause I guess [laughs], 'cause they're deceased. But, you know, they're all addicts. You know, like Johnny Thunders, all these people, you know, whose music I really like, they're all users. So I guess I wanted to try it out anyways. . . . It wasn't like hero worship though. It wasn't like, "I'm gonna get high for [Sex Pistols' bassist] Sid Vicious," you know [laughs]. I mean, I was just curious. . . . I didn't think, "Oh, it killed them," you know, "I shouldn't do it." I was like, thought they, you know, they made like—the New York Dolls made really great music. And the Dead Boys made good music that I liked. So it did—it musta done—something good, you know.

Some study participants attributed their own drug use to the influences of their favorite musicians, but most cited other influences on their decision to use heroin. Many mentioned simple curiosity as a deciding factor. Like the interviewee above, our participants did not want to portray themselves as impressionable individuals who "worshiped" celebrities to the point of using their drugs of choice, but some perceived heroin as a drug used for artistic performance enhancement. A number of admired musicians reportedly created their most acclaimed work in the very depths of their heroin use. Fans who heeded this detail may have regarded heroin as a muse for artistic achievement. While numerous factors were identified as contributing to initiating and continuing heroin use, being a member of such a music-spawned subculture was mentioned repeatedly in relation to heroin and other drug use.

There have been many celebrities highlighted in the media for using heroin, dying from heroin-related deaths, and being arrested for heroin-related charges.

Everybody's Doing It

Nathan, a 23-year-old male heroin "waterliner" (one who liquefies heroin and administers it intranasally), spoke about what attracted him to heroin use. At 13 he ran away from home and started experimenting with drugs. His parents committed him to a mental institution and a juvenile boot camp. He ran away again, initiating heroin use at the age of 17. The interviewer asked Nathan what he had thought about heroin before trying it.

> I wanted to know what it felt like, because, you know all the, all the f***in' famous people do it. There's got to be something to it, you know. F***in' all the people with money f***in' do it. . . . You know, it supposedly, so many people are hooked on it. So I figured it must be somethin' to it. . . . If I'm gonna be a millionaire rock star, I gotta f***in' do [heroin], you know. Everyone else does, sh**. I mean, what are the critics gonna say if I'm not doin' dope? [laughs]

Sarcasm aside, this interviewee raised another important point. There have been many celebrities highlighted in the media for using heroin, dying from heroin-related deaths, and being arrested for heroin-related charges. For Nathan and other aspiring musicians, heroin use seemed like a prerequisite for gaining stardom in the music industry. Nathan repeatedly mentioned wanting to become a successful rock musician, even jokingly linking this goal with heroin use. This outlook is not all that surprising, given the long list of famous rock musicians who at least dabbled in dope and sometimes flirted with death.

A 21-year-old white male, Corey, talked about spending much of his teen years following the Grateful Dead tours. He spoke of these tours as drug havens, where drug use and sales were integral to the Dead show subculture. Corey was asked what it was like touring with the Grateful Dead, and he answered with an evocative smile:

> It was pretty interesting. You meet a lot of stupid people, but you meet cool people too, you know what I mean? I made a lot of money selling drugs, got f***ed up every day. I don't know, that is where I did my first shot of dope at, was at a Dead show. I was 16 or 17, something like that. When I hit (the Dead shows), you could get like anything you wanted, any kind of drug. It was beautiful.

Defiance

A 19-year-old African-American female talked in detail about the heroin use of popular music groups and its impact on young people. Alicia had begun injecting heroin at the age of 14, when "grunge," alternative rock, dominated the MTV scene. Before her heroin initiation, she felt like an outcast in the small, upper-class town where she grew up. Alicia was quick to point out that the media were not the primary reason for her heroin use. Instead, she gave us many thoughtful insights into her decisions to use.

> Well at that time, that was like the time Nirvana came out. I knew a little bit about that. . . . At that time, I mean grungy is the popular culture, and every girl would look at [punk

rock star] Courtney Love and go, "Wow, she's rad!" She is like a rock girl. And that was kind of a cool image. That kind of helped it along and made it not so much the kind of thing you want to cover and really not tell anybody about it. It was like the kind of thing that you would smirk about in class. "Oh yeah, been there, done that." I do think that the media, I mean especially because I read polls or research that has been done. There has been such an explosion of heroin use ever since it fell into mainstream media. They watch Courtney Love and Kurt Cobain, and there are just millions of other bands too that have used forever, and teenagers tend to idolize those people obviously. So there has kind of been a desensitization on the broad front about it. And people have been kind of like, think that it is this trendy habit. However, though, that wasn't the main reason for me. Like I said before, I was just really desperate to escape and to f***ing feel good for once. To be accepted and all those things were kind of rolled up into one when I was going on 14 into 15 and 8th grade. All of a sudden like I could be one of the cooler, cooler people, like the rebel, but still be in my whole familiar territory of the outcasts.

The 'heroin chic' look was created in part by fashion photographer Davide Sorrenti, who overdosed on heroin in 1997 at the age of 20.

Alicia's comments support the notion that media and subculture can powerfully shape a young person's decisions about drug use, and, in this case, heroin use specifically. Alicia's story is also representative of another common characteristic among our participants—defiance. In reporting their initial feelings about heroin, they were often forthcoming and insightful, owning up to their decisions to use. Many of the interviewees sought a socially marginalized status, relating more to outcasts and unconventional types than to the mainstream. . . .

Tragic Beauty

If the "tragic beauty" were to manifest as a visual image, "heroin chic" would best embody it. In the early 1990s the "heroin chic" look was created in part by fashion photographer Davide Sorrenti, who overdosed on heroin in 1997 at the age of 20. Sorrenti, a graffiti artist and opera lover, was part of a heroin-using social world where "high art" and street culture met. To make an aesthetic statement, Sorrenti, followed by other photographers, portrayed waif-like models, with glassy eyes and vapid expressions, in designer clothes. The trend embraced grungy clothing, dark circles under the eyes, pale skin, and poignant, heroin-related imagery. The fashion industry soon realized how powerful a magazine layout could be when several politicians, including President [Bill] Clinton, condemned the look for glamorizing a "strung-out" image. A more healthy, happy look was promoted in subsequent ads and fashion layouts. While "heroin chic" did become popular within the fashion industry, it did not necessarily catch on in popular youth culture. The "heroin chic" style was adopted more often by the alternative rock and "grunge" youth subcultures.

Cameron related the effects of the "heroin chic" portrayed in the media to her continued heroin use. This 20-year-old white female grew up in an upper-middle-class family, and during the interview she disclosed that she had been severely physically abused by her father. When she started to spend time with peers who were using heroin, she felt that they had come together because of the pain they shared. Cameron started using at the age of 16, around 1995, when "heroin chic" had become fashionable. Although her appearance at the time of interview was not reminiscent of "heroin chic," she claimed to still idealize the image.

The problem is so widespread now that it seems like more, it's become more of a mainstream drug. . . . You know, what has changed in the last like 5 to 10 years to make that problem,

I think it's like the biggest consideration, but also the way I think a lot of things associated with heroin are presented to people, as far as like the media goes and other things. . . . It's definitely glamorizing it. Definitely had an effect on me. Like the ultrathin, heroin look with the dark circles and—yeah, it was definitely like, it was something I aimed for at one point, you know? Like I'm still, I try not to make myself think it's attractive, but I still do. . . .

There were many notable testimonies given by our participants regarding their heroin-using lifestyle, their thoughts on media images of heroin, their membership in certain subcultures, and their outlook for the future. While each of these categories can be seen as quite distinct, they are also connected in important ways. Heroin use may have been affected by a negative life outlook, which may have influenced a subculture membership, which may have made particular media portrayals attractive. It also could have worked in the opposite direction, or in both directions at the same time. These retrospective accounts present some exploratory insights into the challenges of disentangling the relationship of youth culture and drug use.

6

Heroin Maintenance Programs Can Reduce Harm to Addicts and Society

David Borden

David Borden is executive director of DRCNet, an organization working for drug policy reform, harm reduction, reform of drug sentencing laws, and medicalization of marijuana and ecstasy.

Heroin addicts face a host of problems that not only impact their own lives but cause problems for society as a whole. Users are often forced to commit crimes to pay for expensive black market heroin. Those who take the drug intravenously often share needles because they have no access to sanitary syringes. Needle sharing is spreading AIDS, hepatitis, and other contagious diseases among users and nonusers alike. To alleviate these problems, officials in Vancouver, Canada, are implementing a program to supply addicts with heroin and syringes in the hopes of steering toward drug treatment and eventual sobriety. Legal access to heroin has shown great benefits in Great Britain, Switzerland, and the Netherlands. Although such programs are controversial, they are the first step in solving the heroin problem and should be implemented on a large scale in both Canada and the United States.

The northern North Americans in Canada are taking another cautious step for drug policy reform. NAOMI, the North American Opiate [Medication Initiative] Project, will

David Borden, "Canada's Cautious First Step," Alternet.org, February 15, 2005. Reproduced by permission.

shortly begin providing maintenance doses of heroin to addicts in Vancouver, moving later to Toronto and Montreal as well. Drug warriors in the U.S. and Canada alike are likely to characterize the project as reckless or wrongheaded. In reality it is a cautious first step only, but an urgently needed one.

In Vancouver's Downtown East Side, where many of the city's hard drug users congregate, the addicted each day face unnecessary levels of risk from overdose, spread of infectious diseases such as hepatitis or HIV, marginalization from society and the health system, a wearing and time-consuming search for money to pay for expensive street drugs, general destabilization of their lives, and all the obstacles to survival, recovery or prosperity these conditions present.

Saving an Entire Generation

Prescription heroin is not a panacea capable of instantly transforming every addict into a happy, productive, model citizen. But the experience of countries such as Switzerland, The Netherlands, Great Britain, even the early 20th-century United States, show that legal access to the drug of choice enables many such people to accomplish that for themselves. The consequences of prohibition are defining and harsh. Counterintuitive though it may seem to some, without prohibition, heroin and even heroin addiction would be markedly less destructive than they are today.

One famous advocate of prescription heroin was Danny Sugerman, long-time manager for the music group the Doors and coauthor of the famous Jim Morrison biography, *No One Here Gets Out Alive*. Danny, who sadly passed away [in January 2005] from cancer, also wrote an amazing book, *Wonderland Avenue: Tales of Glamour and Excess*, telling the story of his descent into serious heroin addiction while living the fast life in West Hollywood. It's the kind of book that you don't want to put down until you've finished it.

Wonderland Avenue made crystal clear that Danny held no illusions about heroin. He keenly understood its dangers—he almost died from them, many close to him did—but he also comprehended the impact of prohibition on addicted drug users. In an interview [in 2001], Danny said, "If you prescribed heroin to current addicts, you'd save an entire generation." Those words were spoken from hard experience and deep thought combined.

We know heroin maintenance works, if carried out in a sound fashion, and the record from other places and times, the people from those places, are there to offer insight and aid.

A Radical Step Forward

In the context of that idea, saving generations of addicts, the NAOMI trial seems much too little—a few or several hundred participants, people who have already tried other therapies unsuccessfully, followed by a weaning off with the potential for a return to the street once the study's done, absent changes in drug policy to permit continuation. Canada has tens of thousands of active heroin users. Doubtless it has to start this way; even in Canada—even in Vancouver—heroin maintenance is a radical step forward, in political terms. But we know heroin maintenance works, if carried out in a sound fashion, and the record from other places and times, the people from those places, are there to offer insight and aid. So amid my satisfaction at this historic step, I cannot forget the uncertainty the future and present alike hold for many, many people who could be saved now.

Still, Canada deserves congratulations—a lot of them—for this cautious but major first step. With favorable results, unceasing pressure, and maybe a little luck, more and larger steps can follow.

7

Heroin Maintenance Programs Do Not Reduce Harm to Addicts and Society

Kevin Sabet

Kevin Sabet was a senior drug-policy speechwriter in the presidential administrations of both Bill Clinton and George W. Bush. He is the author of Dealing with Drugs.

The first program to provide legal access to heroin began in Switzerland in the mid-1980s. Since that time the idea of prescribing heroin to addicts has been promoted in North America and Europe as an answer to the addiction problem. However, studies have shown that legalized heroin programs only allow users to continue their destructive behavior. Heroin addicts need access to counseling and methadone, which can provide relief from opiate addiction. Despite the claims of pro-drug proponents, drug treatment is the only answer to the continuing heroin crisis.

[T]The Canadian city of] Vancouver's latest plan—maintenance for heroin users—overlooks an elementary fact: The problem with drug use is, oddly enough, drug use.

Vancouver has one of the highest rates of drug abuse and infection in the world, according to scientific studies published about the city.

Kevin Sabet, "Why 'Harm Reduction' Won't Work," *The Vancouver Sun*, March 19, 2005. Copyright Vancouver Sun 2005. Reproduced by permission of the author.

That is why Vancouver's latest plan to maintain heroin users on their drugs of choice—cornering more addicts into a life of despair and sickness—is worrying me and scores of public health officials worldwide.

As in most major cities around the world, Vancouver's drug problem is multifaceted and complex: The regular consumption of multiple drugs by a significant minority of the population, rising purity rates, and crippling violence exacerbated by regimented criminal organizations exhaust policy-makers looking for a "quick fix" to the drug problem.

To make matters worse, a disproportionate number of drug addicts in this city have HIV (at least 30 per cent) and Hepatitis C (a staggering 90 per cent), either perpetuated by risky sexual behaviour under the influence of drugs or as a direct result of sharing infected needles.

Even the most extreme anti-drug hawk, then, might be able to understand why so many well-meaning officials and social workers would raise the white flag with policies like government-sponsored drug shooting galleries.

It is astonishing that we must perpetually remind ourselves that drug-taking behaviour can be changed when thousands of people in recovery today are living examples of this truth.

Poor Reviews of Previous Trials

Supporters of these legal injection rooms constantly remind us of the "great Swiss example." Swiss government-funded scientists hailed their heroin maintenance project a success since it concluded that addicts experienced "improvements in health and well-being" and less criminal behaviour. This single review of the Swiss trials has been showcased worldwide as a success of government-sanctioned drug maintenance.

But independent evaluations of the program have been less than sanguine. One of those evaluations—the official line from the United Nations—chided the study on the basis of its shoddy design and poorly drawn conclusions. The World Health Organization concluded that the Swiss studies "have not provided convincing evidence that . . . the medical prescription of heroin generally leads to better outcomes."

Science tells us that heroin maintenance is a sloppy alternative to drug treatment strategies like methadone and buprenorphine. Common sense and compassion dictate that, no matter how difficult, uneasy, or uncomfortable, we cannot hide sufferers of addiction in a drug den on the outskirts of town—we must confront their disease.

It is astonishing that we must perpetually remind ourselves that drug-taking behaviour can be changed when thousands of people in recovery today are living examples of this truth.

So, what is a country or city to do? A lot.

Appropriate Treatment

When Sweden found in 1985 that HIV prevalence was more than 50 per cent in its capital city, it established a comprehensive approach of HIV testing and methadone maintenance treatment coupled with hospital units, drug education and counselling for drug users with infectious diseases.

The result? HIV among injection drug users in that city stands today at five per cent. Drug use there is the lowest in Europe.

Evidence from elsewhere suggests that when the criminal justice system and public health community work together (in the form of specialized "drug courts," for example), our problems get smaller.

Meanwhile, some officials in [Vancouver] still respond to this social and biological disease by prolonging it. HIV and Hepatitis C rates continue to soar; Vancouver's overdose rate is the highest in Canada. One Vancouver police drug squad inspector, Mark Horsley, recently said that Vancouver is the "warehouse distribution centre of drugs in Canada."

Cross-country comparisons are problematic, but giving in to harmful behaviour by supporting drug use gets us nowhere. So-called "harm reduction" measures, no matter how well-intentioned, fail to stop drug use and redirect drug addicts. Instead, these policies accept the inevitability of addiction when we know this disease can be prevented or at least treated.

Reducing total harm, on the other hand, must begin by cutting drug use.

Rejecting heroin maintenance doesn't mean that restrictive drug policies, such as those sanctioned and supported by the UN and U.S., are our magic bullet. They have implementation and effectiveness problems of their own. But our overarching goal should always be to reduce total harm and to make our drug policies work better within that context of reducing drug use.

As elementary as it sounds, it seems that some people still need to be reminded that the problem with drug use is drug use.

A so-called "harm reduction" policy is essentially flawed because it has at its core narrow goals that deny the complex social, legal and biological context of drug use and addiction.

Reducing total harm, then—to one's self, community, and society, users and non-users—must be the true goal of prevention and treatment providers who understand that drug abuse is a treatable, yet fundamentally preventable, disease of the brain and body.

It is inhumane to perpetuate this disease when history and science tell us that it can be prevented and its attendant consequences reduced, if not eliminated.

8

Needle Exchange Programs Slow the Spread of AIDS and Other Diseases

Drug Policy Alliance

The Drug Policy Alliance is the leading organization working to broaden the public debate on drug policy and promote realistic alternatives to drug prohibition and the war on drugs.

More than one out of every three new AIDS cases in the United States can be traced to heroin addicts who share dirty needles. This is a preventable tragedy that can be alleviated by providing sterile syringes to heroin users. Studies have shown that addicts will use clean needles when they are available. However, government officials fighting the war on drugs have opposed clean-needle distribution despite evidence that such programs have multiple benefits to both addicts and society. It is unconscionable that politicians pandering to a fearful public combat clean-needle programs when such opposition only leads to an increase in deadly, contagious diseases such as hepatitis C and HIV.

Increasing the availability of sterile syringes through needle exchange programs, pharmacies, and other outlets reduces unsafe injection practices such as needle sharing, curtails transmission of HIV/AIDS and hepatitis, increases safe

Drug Policy Alliance, "Increasing Access to Sterile Syringes," Drugpolicy.org, May 22, 2006. Reproduced by permission.

disposal of used syringes, and helps injecting drug users obtain drug information, treatment, detoxification, social services, and primary health care.

Injection drug use is associated with high levels of infection of HIV, Hepatitis-C, and various other blood-borne diseases. Injection drug use has accounted, both directly and indirectly, for more than one-third (36%) of AIDS cases in the United States since the epidemic began. Up to seventy-five percent of new AIDS cases among women and children are directly or indirectly a consequence of injection drug use. Zero-tolerance drug policies have outlawed the possession of drug paraphernalia, including syringes, as well as the distribution of sterile syringes (with a few exceptions). These short-sighted policies results in the re-use and sharing of contaminated injection equipment, allowing for the unchecked spread of deadly diseases and the proliferation of poor health conditions.

People of color are disproportionately impacted by the lack of access to sterile syringes. AIDS is the second leading cause of death among African Americans aged 25 to 44 and half of those deaths were caused by injections with contaminated needles. Among Latinos, AIDS is the fourth leading cause of death of those aged 25 to 44 and half of those deaths were caused by injections with contaminated needles.

Saving Lives Three Ways

Syringe availability is therefore critical to saving lives and has been accomplished in three primary ways:

Needle/Syringe Exchange Programs (NEPs) allow people to trade in used syringes for clean needles and have been scientifically proven to greatly reduce the spread of blood-borne diseases. Many states and municipalities in the United States have acted to improve access to sterile syringes. Yet the possession, distribution, and sale of syringes remain a criminal offense in much of the country, and the federal government prohibits the use of its funds for needle exchange programs. This forces many programs offering these important services to operate largely underground. In fact, although there are currently over 140 needle exchange programs in the U.S., they are legal in only 13 states, and that legality often depends on a county-by-county certification of a State of Emergency that must be regularly renewed.

Despite the evidence that needle exchange is one of the most effective strategies of reducing injection-drug-related infections, the federal government refuses to give even one penny to needle exchange programs.

Camden recently became the second city in New Jersey to adopt a life-saving municipal syringe access program. Camden joins Atlantic City, which voted for syringe exchange [in 2004]; the Atlantic County prosecutor filed a lawsuit [several weeks later] to stop Atlantic City from implementing the program. . . .

Pharmacy Sale of Syringes—where pharmacies are permitted to sell syringes over the counter similar to other medical equipment—remains illegal in most states. However, a growing number of states are enacting laws to allow the pharmacy sale of syringes. Since Connecticut reformed their drug paraphernalia and prescription laws to allow pharmacy sales in 1992, needle sharing among injecting drug users dropped by 40%. In 2000, New York, New Hampshire, and Rhode Island joined the majority of states in allowing pharmacy sales of sterile syringes. California is amongst the states currently considering permitting pharmacy sale of syringes.

Physician Prescription of Syringes. Another means of providing increased access to sterile syringes is by permitting doctors to prescribe syringes to their patients. This would appear to be uncontroversial—recognizing the appropriate role of doctors in preventing the spread of disease—yet few states currently allow this practice. . . . Like needle exchange programs, physician prescription of syringes provides a vehicle through which intravenous drug users can access health care and other basic services. These programs are also important sources of referral to drug treatment programs.

Misguided War on Drugs

While the United States is one of the largest funders of AIDS prevention in the world and despite the evidence that needle exchange is one of the most effective strategies of reducing injection-drug-related infections, the federal government refuses to give even one penny to needle exchange programs.

Under the aegis of the "War on Drugs," many government agencies and politicians have sought to eliminate needle exchanges and other health service providers for drug users, through both legal and illegal means. While some law enforcement agencies recognize the benefits of needle exchange programs, there are far too many examples of police harassing needle exchange workers and their clients, and working to eliminate these important public health programs. Litigation on behalf of needle exchange program clients in Bridgeport, CT successfully challenged such police harassment against a needle exchange program. Another similar case is currently underway in Massachusetts, where local police forces have arrested needle exchange participants despite a statewide public health initiative allowing pilot programs in certain towns across the state.

9

Methadone Is Nearly as Deadly as Heroin

Theodore Dalrymple

*Theodore Dalrymple is a British psychiatrist and author of
numerous books, including* Our Culture, What's Left of It: The
Mandarins and the Masses *and* Life at the Bottom: The
Worldview That Makes the Underclass.

*Methadone is a deadly drug that kills nearly as many people as
heroin. While the synthetic narcotic is often promoted as a way
to treat addiction, methadone is not always taken by heroin addicts. Instead, addicts obtain large quantities of methadone from
drug treatment programs and sell it on the black market. Those
who buy the drug on the street can easily overdose because they
have little physical tolerance to the powerful narcotic. Occasionally, children of drug users are poisoned when they take
methadone pills left in the open. To stop this slaughter, govern-
ments must only hand out a single daily dose of methadone and
insist that addicts ingest the drug in the presence of medical
personnel or drug counselors. To do less is to provide a license to
kill to every doctor who prescribes methadone to heroin addicts.*

The British government is bribing doctors to kill their
patients and others. It wants (and will pay them) to
prescribe methadone to heroin addicts, in the full knowledge

that this will be done in so sloppy and irresponsible a fashion that many people will die as a result. He who wills the means, wills the ends.

The arguments for the prescription of methadone to heroin addicts are well known. Methadone is a synthetic opiate first developed in Nazi Germany during [World War II] because of a shortage of opium supplies from the Far East. It was named dolophine in honour of a leader of the time [Adolph Hitler] (it is still sold under a similar brand name in the United States), and one of its first recipients was Hermann Goering, an addict whose criminality was not much reduced by its prescription.

In Florida in 2001, deaths from methadone poisoning surpassed those from heroin poisoning for the first time, by 133 to 121.

Methadone is given mainly in liquid form, though it also exists as a pill and an injection, as a substitute for heroin. Its effects are long-lasting by comparison with those of heroin, so that it is taken only once a day. The rationale behind methadone treatment of drug addicts is that its prescription free of charge reduces the criminal activities of addicts, reduces their consumption of heroin and hence their risk-taking behaviour, and stabilises their day-to-day existence so that they are able to rejoin society, while eventually allowing them painlessly to reduce the dose little by little until they achieve total abstinence. Controlled trials have demonstrated the beneficial effects of methadone for groups of addicts.

Unfortunately, methadone is a very dangerous drug. Five millilitres [ml]—a teaspoonful—is enough to kill a baby, and 40ml is enough to kill an adult who is not habituated to opiates. The dangers are not merely theoretical, not even for the doctors who prescribe the stuff: From time to time one reads in the medical press of doctors who have been struck off the medical register for negligently believing the lies their patients tell them about the amount of methadone they take, amounts that promptly kill their patients.

Black Market Methadone Sales

Deaths from methadone are by no means negligible in number. In Florida in 2001, deaths from methadone poisoning surpassed those from heroin poisoning for the first time, by 133 to 121. Meanwhile, [in Great Britain], to demonstrate that we are also in the vanguard of modernity, deaths from methadone have been rising steadily. Between 1993 and 2000, there were 4,058 deaths from the direct effects of heroin; in the same period, there were 2,500 deaths from methadone. Since far fewer than a third of addicts receive methadone, it is at least as likely, to put it no stronger, that methadone kills rather than saves.

A large percentage of those who die of methadone poisoning are not those who are prescribed it, but purchasers of methadone from those who receive it free and use the proceeds to buy heroin (and sometimes children of addicts who are attracted to the bright green sweet liquid). Diversion of methadone on to the black market is so widespread that the price is low: currently about £1 [$1.75] for 10ml. Addicts are able to sell their methadone because they are prescribed bottles of it at a time.

The diversion of this dangerous substance on to the black market—where it kills—hardly gives our distinguished government pause, or slows the self-propelled juggernaut of the drug addiction treatment industry. And there could be no clearer illustration of how those who work in the field of drug addiction have become a self-serving bureaucracy than the response of an Australian in the field to the fact that in New South Wales 46 per cent of those who die of methadone poisoning have never been prescribed it: "The large proportion of deaths involving diverted methadone may suggest a high unmet demand for methadone and/or a need to make methadone maintenance treatment attractive to a greater diversity of dependent heroin users." As a physician friend of mine at the hospital in which I work remarked (where, incidentally, we have treated 51 methadone overdoses [between late 2001 and early 2003], many requiring intensive care), this is a little like concluding from the existence of rape that there is an unmet demand for sex.

As it happens, it is not inevitable that the prescription of methadone must be accompanied by so many deaths. In Glasgow, [Scotland,] for instance, the number of people prescribed methadone increased from 140 in 1992 to 2,800 in 1998. But the number of deaths from methadone in the city increased from three to seven, that is to say they declined proportionately by 86 per cent.

The rise in deaths from methadone in America is probably attributable to the adoption of British methods . . . with predictably disastrous results.

Tantamount to Murder

The reason for this was obvious: Glasgow instituted a policy according to which those prescribed methadone had to take it in front of the dispensing pharmacist each day, and were not given a supply that they could turn into cash. Ninety per cent of methadone prescriptions were dispensed in this fashion; if it had been 100 per cent, the deaths would have been even fewer. Clearly, this method of prescription must have been acceptable to addicts, since so many of them agreed to it.

These figures suggest, indeed, that it is the only ethically acceptable method of prescription; all other methods are tantamount to murder, or at least culpable homicide. Yet the latter methods will remain predominant for the foreseeable future, as most places have not instituted the Glaswegian approach. The death of a drug addict or one of those people inclined to buy methadone on the black market probably saves the British taxpayer a considerable sum of money in the long run, or even the short run, but this is surely taking the desirable principle of economising where possible a little far. Incidentally, the rise in deaths from methadone in America is probably attributable to the adoption of British methods. For once, the Americans are copying us, with predictably disastrous results.

With [methadone] treatment, we end up with a methadone addict and a heroin addict, whereas before we had only a heroin addict.

There is another, wider objection to methadone maintenance treatment, however—or indeed any form of treatment of drug addicts. It is astonishing to me that the authors of trials which demonstrate a reduction of criminality among addicts when prescribed methadone conclude that the prescription of methadone will reduce the total amount of allegedly drug-fuelled crime in society.

Not only is the relationship between criminality and drug-taking much more complex than the "feed-my-habit" conception usually peddled (the decision to take heroin is also a conscious way of opting for the criminal life, because no one any longer is ignorant of the consequences of taking the drug), but it does not follow that, if criminality is reduced among treated addicts, criminality as a whole decreases.

The New Wretched of the Earth

If you were a drug dealer with a customer who told you that, thanks to methadone (or any other treatment), you no longer required his wares, would you simply accept the contraction of your market, or would you act as any salesman would act when one customer fails to buy? Thus, it is possible that, with treatment, we end up with a methadone addict and a heroin addict, whereas before we had only a heroin addict.

Does this fit what has actually happened in Britain better than, say, the tuberculosis [TB] model of methadone treatment? When a patient has infectious TB, treating him is not only therapeutic for him but preventive for the public: It interrupts the transmission of the disease. But the apparatus of treatment for drug addiction is more likely to spread the problem—I won't call it a disease—than to cure or prevent it. The number of people receiving methadone in [Great Britain] has reached 30,000, but heroin continues to cut a swathe through the lower reaches of society. Opium (loosely construed) has become the opium of the masses.

Neither methadone nor any other medicalised "treatment" will solve the social problem of heroin addiction. On the contrary, it will increase it. True, a doctor has to do his best for the individual patient who consults him: He treats an individual's problems, not those of society and therefore can quite ethically, on the basis of published research, come to the conclusion that methadone is the best available solution to his patient's current problem—provided that the methadone is swallowed in front of a pharmacist. It is not his concern if, by prescribing the wretched stuff, he is encouraging the spread of heroin yet further.

Speaking to hundreds of addicts, as I do, it is evident that, considered as a whole, the problem is a deep social, psychological, cultural, moral, educational and spiritual one. There is no technical fix for it, not now and not in the future. Biomedical research, however fascinating it may be from the point of view of disinterested intellectual curiosity, will not provide a solution.

The poor abandoned addicts whom I see every day of my life have never had a father, have never eaten a meal at a table with other people, have nothing in their minds but pop music and football. They are the new wretched of the earth, and there is no medicine for their wretchedness.

10

Buprenorphine Can Cure Heroin Addiction

Dannie Martin

Dannie Martin is coauthor of Committing Journalism: The Prison Writings of Red Hog *and has two published novels,* The Dishwasher *and* In the Hat. *He is a former bank robber and heroin addict who kicked his habit with buprenorphine.*

Heroin addiction is an expensive habit that often forces users to rob banks or commit other crimes. Many addicts only quit when forced to go cold turkey, or give up abruptly, in prison. Upon release, many begin taking heroin again. However, a new anti-heroin drug called buprenorphine is allowing addicts to quit heroin easily. Unlike methadone, which is nearly as addictive as heroin, buprenorphine, or bupre, is an instant cure. The drug has no high or withdrawal symptoms associated with it. Former addicts who have been cured by bupre agree that this amazing drug can provide relief and thus benefit users and society alike.

A new drug approved [in 2002] to treat heroin addiction is gaining acceptance, and I say it's about time. I'm a former bank robber and ex-heroin addict who kicked his habit years ago with the help of the drug, which was experimental then. But you should be hearing a lot more about it now.

Dane Martin, "New Anti-Heroin Drug Saved My Health and Maybe a Few Banks," *Pacific News Service*, May 22, 2003. Reproduced by permission of New America Media.

The Federal Drug Administration [Food and Drug Administration] approved buprenorphine hydrochloride [in October 2002]. Now, doctors associated with the Haight-Ashbury Free Medical Clinic in San Francisco have announced they will use it to help addicts get through withdrawals.

We heroin addicts dread going through withdrawal. For some, going cold turkey in prison has been the only way to finally kick heroin. But by then, they may have left behind countless victims as they tried to feed the habit.

Over a quarter of a century ago, methadone was introduced for the maintenance of heroin addicts. As it turns out, methadone's high is as potent as heroin's, and most addicts find it even harder to kick. Now there is a whole new crop of methadone addicts who use heroin as a fallback.

A Painless Cure

In 1992, buprenorphine was in the experimental stage and not approved for treatment. That year, I again took up heroin after being paroled from a bank robbery conviction for which I did 12 years. My habit was spiraling out of control and the future was looking bleak.

It was the first habit I had ever kicked in my long life of addiction outside of jail.

Then a [San Francisco] Bay Area doctor I knew, through some barely legal shenanigans, got me a prescription for buprenorphine. He wasn't sure if it would work, but thought it had potential. My desperation to kick heroin after 45 years of on-and-off use and my lack of future prospects made it worth a shot.

Only one local pharmacy handled buprenorphine at the time, dispensing it in little gelatin squares like chewing gum. The theory is that the drug goes to the same receptors in the brain as opiates do, and blocks them off.

I took the dosage, stopped shooting up heroin and felt nothing. By nothing, I mean I felt no high and no withdrawal symptoms, either. After one week my habit was gone—without the chills, sweats, severe nausea, dry heaves, diarrhea, horrible muscle cramps, extreme anxiety and sleeplessness that characterize heroin withdrawal as the body comes back to life.

It was the first habit I had ever kicked in my long life of addiction outside of jail. The drug may have spared my life and a few banks at the same time.

Over 75 percent of the bank robbers I met in prison were heroin addicts who turned to robbing banks to feed their habits. After a successful robbery they could afford more drugs than before. So they increased their habit. That increased the horror of the prospect of withdrawal, which increased their will to rob. A vicious circle, littered with victims.

Buprenorphine was a miracle drug. . . . It helped me clear my habit, and it can't be abused.

Cautious Optimism

Buprenorphine's possible side effects are said to include cold and flu-like symptoms, headaches, nausea, sweating and mood swings. I did not experience any of these. If combined with alcohol, it can cause death from respiratory problems.

Clinicians at Haight-Ashbury are expressing cautious optimism about the drug, noting that it doesn't work for some people and stressing that complex problems like drug addiction have no one-shot cure. Some doctors elsewhere say buprenorphine works for only a few.

But for me, buprenorphine was a miracle drug. I credit it with starting me down the path to sobriety, showing me that painless heroin withdrawal was a possibility. It helped me clear my habit, and it can't be abused because there is no high.

Buprenorphine has the potential to significantly lower the number of crimes committed by frantic heroin addicts, and could help reduce the startling number of inmates in American prisons on drug-related convictions.

11

Ibogaine Can Cure Heroin Addiction

Sebastian Horsley

Sebastian Horsley is a British artist, author, and former heroin addict.

Heroin users are turning to ibogaine, a powerful drug, to help them fight addiction. Traditionally taken as a religious sacrament by members of the Bwiti tribe in Gabon, Africa, the plant-based ibogaine causes users to experience extremely intense visions and bizarre hallucinations. Although no one knows how it works, most heroin addicts who take ibogaine are able to stop using opiates immediately after the hallucinogen wears off. Although ibogaine is another dangerous drug, it has helped thousands of addicts find a cure for addiction.

As I started to feel the effects of the drug I was suddenly seized with fear. I had taken a hallucinogenic which could confuse the dreaming and waking states, my adulthood and childhood, and in doing so break the cellophane between myself and insanity. Sometimes drugs have been a trip into the horrors of my life and sometimes a means of flight from them. But nightmares are never more horrific than real life. Are they?

Perhaps I shouldn't have worried. As a child I saw everything as a novelty—I was always intoxicated. Alcoholism didn't run in my family, it galloped. By the time I was in my teens I was already sluicing down liquor with the abandon of someone truly spooked by his own existence. And it went on from there.

By the time I was 30, crack had taken me, as swiftly and easily as an eagle taking a rabbit. Crack led to heroin: first smoking, then the needle. I took drugs as an escape from a life which I found unendurable. I took drugs because I enjoyed taking them. The fixing [shooting heroin] ritual is the sweetest form of pleasure a man can have. The needle, the belt round the arm, the first feeling of the spike sliding through the flesh . . . The ecstasy of hitting a vein is incomparably pleasurable. Complete happiness is about to be yours. You hear the angels sing. You feel the kiss of God. The whole world is bathed in the luminous glow of entrancement, of contentment, of peace.

Those who have never taken drugs can't understand this bliss. How could I ever give up? It wasn't just the pleasure, it was my life. I had always been absorbed by the idea of the decadents—by those doomed visionaries, strutting peacocks possessed of an arrogant lust for life. I wanted to wear their outlaw colours. I wanted to share their fearlessness. Some see addiction as weakness. But for me it was a strength. It was the strength to lose control, to run counter to convention, to escape the banal confines of what I saw as bourgeois life.

Of course, the heroics couldn't last. In the end, taking crack and heroin is about as glamorous as swigging meths [drinking cleaning solvents]. The irony of the drug experience is that it comes from an outgrowth of genuine longing, a reaching out for meaning, a yearning for transcendence and salvation, and it ends with sitting in a darkened room staring miserably at the wall.

I had wanted freedom, but all I had made was a prison. Just as I can't describe the pleasure of drug taking, I can't describe the dead end of loneliness, of abandonment, of the boredom that it led to. So I tried to give up. Then I gave up giving up. The relapses were endless and tedious and sad.

No Pleasure Trip

I was like an escapologist who messes up his tricks and gets even more tangled. My life was an ongoing flight. I guess in a way my on/off relationship with drugs was an external expression of my internal struggle. I tried clinics, I tried Narcotics Anonymous, I tried therapy, reduction cures, exercise and, eventually, sheer white-knuckled denial. I had multiple stabs at rehab, and sometimes I managed for maybe a month, maybe more. Finally, I even got as far as a year—quickly followed by a four-month relapse. I was exhausted. I couldn't see a way out of my predicament. I wanted to want to stop. But I couldn't get over my cravings. And so I would come to the conclusion that if I was thinking about drugs that much I might as well take them. And so I did. But this time I decided that the drug would be ibogaine.

Among ibogaine takers, four (recorded) deaths have occurred suspiciously close to the time the drug was tried.

I had been reading about ibogaine for some years. And I think, to be honest, I had been put off it for the simple reason that I was afraid—afraid it might work. Who would I be without my addiction? If I kicked out my devils would my angels leave, too? Without my caricature to hide in, how could I find a disguise? I was frightened that I had become a self-parody—but without going to the trouble of acquiring a self first.

The time had come to find out. After a grand finale of a relapse which left me more dead than alive, I contacted an ibogaine treatment provider who I had traced through the internet. She was called Hattie Wells and she said she could supply me with the drug at an affordable price and help me go through the experience. 'This is no pleasure trip,' she warned.

It's not a small task. I had to go to my doctor for blood tests and heart scans to check I was up to it. I was advised to take a week or two off work. I had taken my life off already so that was no problem. Then I had to suggest somewhere I could go, a quiet place where I felt safe. Some people go to clinics abroad, in a controlled medical environment. I chose my girlfriend's house.

But even there I desperately wanted to cancel at the last minute. I had reacquired a heroin habit from my last relapse. I didn't feel emotionally capable. I was frightened of dying—among ibogaine takers, four (recorded) deaths have occurred suspiciously close to the time the drug was tried. And even more suspicious were my own motives: taking drugs to stop taking drugs. Yeah right, that's a new one.

All my self-consciousness was swept away by the sheer force and intensity of the visions.

Hattie arrived with a doctor who gave me a medical and I signed a form exonerating her from any liability. Then, after a test dose to check that I wasn't allergic, I took a gel-capped extract of the rootbark powder.

Lucid Dreaming

Hattie led me up to my room. She put a bucket by the bed in case I vomited. And I lay down feeling excited, but nervous. I didn't know where I was going, but I was on my way. And there was no going back. And then . . . well, nothing much. After an hour of waiting for the sudden drug rush that I had learnt to expect, I felt nothing. A little light-headed perhaps, but nothing dramatic. And then I shut my eyes. And that was it. Sudden images began to emerge out of the darkness like staccato flashes from a film screen. The first was a woman on a raft smiling inanely as she came towards me. I was sceptical at first—you're not fooling me with this, I thought. This is not real. But then all my self-consciousness was swept away by the sheer force and intensity of the visions.

It was a bit like going down into an echoing cathedral, a yawning underworld. But at the same time it was like being inside a miniature jewellery box. Everything was tiny and winking and gleaming and plush. And my head was filled with a buzzing noise, like a telephone line that has been disconnected. And then, immediately—inevitably—I was back, running about amid my childhood. I was at High Hall in Yorkshire, where I had been brought up.

Face pressed against a window, I watched my mother and my sister inside the study running round and round in circles. I don't know who was chasing who, but even at the time I took it to mean something about their relationship, eternally unresolved. But I felt that there was nothing that could be done, that I couldn't interfere.

Then I was flying, soaring over the gardens. It was like lucid dreaming—when you know that you are dreaming and can somehow control your fantasies. But the drug was going to control the visions, not me.

I was strangely aware I was not alone. I heard voices. They could have been simply manifestations of the mind, but at the same time I was aware of the presence of some sort of guide, the spirit of Igoba, the Africans call it. It comes to you as a teacher.

I wanted to swoop through the front door and into the house. It wouldn't let me. It kept dragging me round to the side. 'Everything you need to know is at the side door,' it kept saying.

After the trip, Hattie quoted [Colombian novelist] Gabriel Garcia Marquez to me: 'I have learned that everyone wants to live on the peak of the mountain, without knowing that the real happiness is in how it is scaled.' This made sense to me. I have spent my life going for the hit, the big experience, the extreme situation. I have always needed a drama from time to time to remind me that I still existed. Was this telling me that I could discover beauty in ordinary things? That I didn't always have to take centre stage, to be hopping up and down in an attempt to get noticed? I could slip back into my life through a quiet side door. My reading, for what it is worth, is that Iboga was trying to teach me that all men are ordinary men—the extraordinary men are those who know it.

Bizarre Visions

I can't remember the order in which everything happened. But I remember having a vision about my brother with whom my relationship had always been fraught—the usual sibling rivalries carried to some pretty nasty and petty extremes. He was, after all, a potential threat to my individuality. We like to speak casually about 'sibling rivalry' as though it were some kind of by-product of growing up, a bit of competitiveness and selfishness in children who have been spoilt, who haven't yet grown into a generous social nature. But it is too all-absorbing and relentless to be an aberration; it expresses the heart of the creature—the desire to stand out. Now, suddenly, I saw that the war was over. We flew together until we faced each other. I took off my head. He took off his.

A junkie wouldn't treat a dog the way he treats himself.

I placed mine on his shoulders and he placed his on mine. I have to say that I think he got the better deal. But all the time I was aware of some brooding presence—something that was waiting for me, something I would have to face. It was underneath the surface of everything, glowing away to itself. It was time to face my addiction. I started my journey, soaring and swooping, plunging and diving through forests and mountains and oceans and galaxies. It felt like forever. And then suddenly I was in an opulent room. The sort where kings banquet in fairy-tale castles. I was waiting for an audience with someone—some god who would reveal everything to me. It was an utter inevitability. I waited, resigned.

Then the door swung open . . . and I walked in. I got up to meet myself. I walked slowly towards me and kissed myself on the lips. And as I did so the other me disintegrated, crumbled away like a china doll. I stepped forward to find it again. It was gone.

This was the end of the road. No more excuses. No more psychobabble. No more alibis. Father didn't love me? So what. I'm a failure? Who cares. If you simply put heroin down you are avoiding the issue. It wasn't the horse [a nickname for heroin]. It was the Horsley. It had been me all along.

A Flick of a Switch

Well, now it was over. Now it was time to be a man. A junkie wouldn't treat a dog the way he treats himself. And if I had ever believed—as I had—that people are far more interesting if they don't learn to love themselves, then it was time at least to try and change. I expect that I can't. I don't know where I would be without grandiose self-loathing.

But the main thing I realised was the unbearable lightness of addiction. The ball and chain had floated off, light as a feather. It was as simple as the flick of a switch. You just put 'No' where 'Yes' used to be. So much of my connection with life had always been with the dark side. But throughout my trip I was aware that my death was always with me. I didn't have to run around looking for it. I didn't have to open that door any more. I wanted to ask Iboga where I would go instead, and I was shown an image of myself and my girlfriend with a child between us. I have never had a paternal stirring in my life, no desire to breed misfit freaks like myself, so I found this alarming.

After taking ibogaine I was overwhelmed with a feeling that something good had happened.

Of course, I can only remember a tiny part of my journey, a few snatched fragments of images—perhaps those that meant the most? I opened my eyes. I guessed that maybe 15 minutes had passed. I saw the room through a veil. Hattie was sitting on the floor by the bed.

'You were under for more than nine hours,' she said. She told me that my trip had been one of the most acutely physical that she had witnessed. I had been shaking spasmodically, making weird breathing noises. My arms and hands had assumed infantile gestures for much of the trip.

This tallied with my feelings that I had been involved in some sort of exorcism. I don't believe in spirits, even if they do exist, but I had a real sense that my body had been emptied out. It felt like I had had a blood transfusion, like a benign force had come to help me. That was a complete contrast to the drugs I had been used to taking. Hallucinogens may often be considered sacred—there are peyote cults and bannisteria cults, hashish and mushroom cults—but no one ever suggested that heroin is holy.

There are no high priests of crack. These drugs are profane, pernicious. When you are in the grip of them you could almost imagine you are under some diabolic possession. When you come down you are swamped with guilt and self-loathing. But after taking ibogaine I was overwhelmed with a feeling that something good had happened. I felt that my brain had been reset. Maybe it is a case of things having to be believed to be seen, but throughout the trip there was a buzzing and fizzing and popping in my head, almost as if nerve endings were being sorted, reconnected, cleaned and ordered into parallel lines like the ploughing of a field.

Suicidal, Centered, and Calm

Trying to explain my insights, they start to sound obvious or silly or indulgent. But that wasn't how they felt at the time. They felt profound, almost divine, delivered with great weight and authority.

I am cynical by nature. Spirituality seems to me to be a form of drug pushing. Our age is a hysterical hot zone of trumped up disorders, imaginary illnesses, panic attacks. We are abducted by aliens. We recall false memories. Truth wears a thousand different faces. Religion is an accident of geography. Nothing more. Nothing less.

The most extraordinary thing is that my craving for drugs has disappeared—completely, and yet in a quiet way.

My ibogaine treatment was the same. It can be interpreted according to any belief system. It could be reincarnation, astral travel, a shamanistic trip. For me it was merely a chemical substance that made me feel a certain way. And the way I felt was that I had been emotionally reintroduced to myself. It was as simple—and as complicated—as that.

Afterwards I didn't sleep for two days. I burst into tears all the time. I think it felt like mourning. I was confused for a week or two. I didn't recognise who I was. I used to be woken every morning with stimulants so that I could drift through the day on sedatives. But now what? Hattie had told me not to worry, to 'find glory in dismemberment'. But I didn't like it.

It is now more than three months since I took it. After a while I began to notice that I didn't need as much sleep as I used to. Apparently this is typical. For most of my life I have been plagued by obsessive compulsive disorder. I have been a slave to endless rituals—touching and counting—all to keep control, to stave off the chaos I sensed inside myself. Sometimes these rituals were occupying two hours a day. And now they had all but disappeared. I still feel sad—a melancholy that is probably part of my character. Clean, my outlook remains deathlike, as it was on drugs. On heroin. Off heroin. I am essentially suicidal. But at the same time I feel centred and calm. And that's new.

But the most extraordinary thing is that my craving for drugs has disappeared—completely, and yet in a quiet way. In the past I always came out of clinics with all guns blazing, on the so-called 'pink cloud'. If I could take drugs like a demon then I could go straight like a demon. It never worked.

This time I feel I have replaced the habit of using drugs with the habit of not using drugs, but gently. The whisper can be louder than the shout. I don't for one moment regret the drugs I have taken. If I had to live my life again, I'd take the same drugs, only sooner. And more of them.

But now I hope it's over. I'm excited. It's some time since I've been excited about anything except the arrival of my dealer. I'm not sure that things ever get lighter, it's just that we become accustomed to the dark. But I shall try. Now I've tasted the bitter root of drug addiction, I'm hoping the fruit will be sweet.

Organizations to Contact

American Council for Drug Education (ACDE)
164 West Seventy-fourth St.
New York, NY 10023
(800) 488-DRUG (3784) • fax: (212) 595-2553
e-mail: acde@phoenixhouse.org
Web site: www.acde.org

The ACDE informs the public about the harmful effects of abusing drugs and alcohol. It gives the public access to scientifically based, compelling prevention programs and materials. ACDE has resources for parents, youth, educators, prevention professionals, employers, health-care professionals, and other concerned community members who are working to help America's youth avoid the dangers of drug and alcohol abuse.

Cato Institute
1000 Massachusetts Ave. NW
Washington, DC 20001-5403
(202) 842-0200 • fax: (202) 842-3490
Web site: www.cato.org

The Cato Institute is a nonprofit libertarian public policy research foundation that seeks to broaden the parameters of public policy debate to allow consideration of the traditional American principles of limited government, individual liberty, free markets, and opposition to the war on drugs. The institute researches issues in the media and provides commentary for magazine, newspaper, and news show editorials.

Drug Enforcement Administration (DEA)
2401 Jefferson Davis Hwy.
Alexandria, VA 22301
(202) 305-8500
Web site: www.dca.gov

The mission of the DEA is to enforce the controlled substances laws and regulations of the United States and bring to the criminal and civil justice system of the United States those involved in the growing, manufacture, or distribution of controlled substances. The DEA also recommends and supports nonenforcement public education programs aimed at reducing the availability of illicit controlled substances on the domestic and international markets. In addition to providing information about illicit drugs on its Web site, the DEA publishes the monthly newsletter *Microgram Bulletin*, primarily intended to assist and serve forensic scientists concerned with the detection and analysis of suspected controlled substances for forensic/law enforcement purposes.

Drug Policy Alliance
925 Fifteenth St. NW, 2nd Floor
Washington, DC 20005
(202) 216-0035 • fax: (202) 216-0803
e-mail: dc@drugpolicy.org
Web site: www.drugpolicy.org

Drug Policy Alliance seeks to broaden public debate on drug policy and to promote realistic alternatives to the war on drugs that are based on science, compassion, health, and human rights. The Drug Policy Alliance is guided by the belief that there are steps that can and should be taken to reduce the harms associated with both drug use and the failed drug war, including making marijuana legally available for medical purposes, curtailing drug testing, redirecting most government drug control resources from criminal justice and interdiction to public health and education, supporting effective science-based drug education and ending support for ineffective programs, and repealing mandatory minimum sentences for nonviolent drug offenses. The online Drug Policy Alliance library is one of the largest collections on drugs and drug policies in the world. It contains over ten thousand books, reports, government documents, periodicals, videos, and articles from the United States and abroad as well as in-depth collections on drug-related policies in Canada, Latin America, and Europe.

Drug Prevention Network of the Americas (DPNA)
119 N. Sixth St., Suite 203
Alpine, TX 79830
(432) 364-0016 • fax: (432) 364-0023
Web site: http://dpna.org

The DPNA is a nonprofit corporation committed to drug education and the prevention of drug abuse. DPNA is a coalition of nongovernment organizations from North and South America working cooperatively to reduce the demand for illicit drugs. DPNA publishes antidrug brochures, policy publications, and books such as *Drug Prevention Advice for Parents*.

Drug Reform Coordination Network (DRCNet)
1623 Connecticut Ave. NW, 3rd Floor
Washington, DC 20009
(202) 293-8340 • fax: (202) 293-8344
e-mail: drcnet@drcnet.org
Web site: www.stopthedrugwar.org

The DRCNet was founded in 1993 and has grown into an international body that includes parents, educators, students, lawyers, health-care professionals, academics, and others working for drug policy reform. The network advocates harm reduction, reform of sentencing and forfeiture laws, legalizing drugs such as marijuana and ecstasy for medical purposes, and promotion of an open debate on drug prohibition. DRCNet opposes filling prisons with drug offenders and supports alternative policies consistent with the principles of peace, justice, freedom, compassion, and truth. The network's online drug policy library contains hundreds of documents relating to drug prohibition. It also publishes a weekly newsletter, *Drug War Chronicle*, available through e-mail subscription.

The National Alliance of Advocates for Buprenorphine Treatment (NAABT)
PO Box 333
Farmington, CT 06034
fax: (860) 269-4391
e-mail: makecontact@naabt.org
Web site: www.naabt.org

The NAABT is a nonprofit organization formed to help heroin users find treatment providers who are willing and able to treat heroin dependency with buprenorphine under a doctor's supervision. The organization publishes brochures, news articles, true stories, and audio files concerning buprenorphine treatment.

National Center on Addiction and Substance Abuse at Columbia University (CASA)
633 Third Ave., 19th Floor
New York, NY 10017-6706
(212) 841-5200 • fax: (212) 956-8020
Web site: www.casacolumbia.org

CASA is a private nonprofit organization that works to educate the public about the costs and hazards of substance abuse and the prevention and treatment of all forms of chemical dependency. The center supports treatment as the best way to reduce chemical dependency. The Policy Research and Analysis division of CASA produces publications such as *Family Matters: Substance Abuse and the American Family* that describe the harmful effects of alcohol and drug addiction and effective ways to address the problem of substance abuse.

National Institute on Drug Abuse (NIDA)
6001 Executive Blvd., Room 5213
Bethesda, MD 20892-9561

(301) 443-1124
e-mail: information@lists.nida.nih.gov
Web site: www.nida.nih.gov

NIDA's mission is to use the power of science to stop drug abuse and addiction. In pursuing this mission, NIDA supports over 85 percent of the world's research on the health aspects of drug abuse and addiction. This ranges from molecular research to the efficacy of managed care and outreach programs. NIDA utilizes new technologies to further the understanding of how drugs affect the brain and behavior. It also strives to ensure the rapid and effective transfer of scientific data to policy makers, health-care practitioners, and the general public. The organization's publications catalog is available online and contains documents relating to basic research, the nature and extent of drug abuse, causes of drug abuse and addiction, HIV/AIDS, drug abuse treatment, and preventing drug abuse.

Students for Sensible Drug Policy (SSDP)
1623 Connecticut Ave. NW, Suite 300
Washington, DC 20009
(202) 293-4414 • fax: (202) 293-8344
e-mail: ssdp@ssdp.org
Web site: www.ssdp.org

The SSDP neither encourages nor condemns drug use. Instead, the organization was founded to provide information about the harm it believes is caused by the war on drugs. The group works to involve young people in the political process and promotes an open, honest, and rational discussion of alternative solutions to the nation's drug problems.

Bibliography

Books

Caroline Jean Acker — *Creating the American Junkie: Addiction Research in the Classic Era of Narcotic Control*. Baltimore: Johns Hopkins University Press, 2002.

Charles Bowden — *A Shadow in the City: Confessions of an Undercover Drug Warrior*. Orlando, FL: Harcourt, 2005.

William S. Burroughs — *Junky: The Definitive Text of "Junk."* New York: Penguin, 2003.

Tom Carnwath and Ian Smith — *Heroin Century*. New York: Routledge, 2002.

Ross Coomber and Nigel South, eds. — *Drug Use and Cultural Contexts "Beyond the West": Tradition, Change and Post-colonialism*. London: Free Association, 2004.

David T. Courtwright — *Dark Paradise: A History of Opiate Addiction in America*. Cambridge, MA: Harvard University Press, 2001.

David Coutright, Herman Joseph, and Don Des Jarlais — *Addicts Who Survive*. Knoxville: University of Tennessee Press, 1989.

Dave Dhaval — *Illicit Drug Use Among Arrestees and Drug Prices*. Cambridge, MA: National Bureau of Economic Research, 2004.

Jennifer Friedman and Marixsa Alicea	*Surviving Heroin: Interviews with Women in Methadone Clinics.* Gaincsvillc: University Press of Florida, 2001.
Jim Hogshire	*Opium for the Masses.* Port Townsend, WA: Loompanics, 1994.
James A. Inciardi	*The War on Drugs III: The Continuing Saga of the Mysteries and Miseries of Intoxication, Addiction, Crime, and Public Policy.* Boston: Allyn & Bacon, 2002.
James A. Inciardi and Lana D. Harrison, eds.	*Heroin in the Age of Crack-Cocaine.* Thousand Oaks, CA: Sage, 1998.
Robert M. Julien	*A Primer of Drug Action.* New York: Freeman, 1996.
Dean Latimer and Jeff Goldberg	*Flowers in the Blood: The Story of Opium.* New York: Franklin Watts, 1981.
Alfred W. McCoy	*The Politics of Heroin: CIA Complicity in the Global Drug Trade; Afghanistan, Southeast Asia, Central America, Colombia.* Chicago: Lawrence Hill, 2003.
T.H. Metzger	*The Birth of Heroin and the Demonization of the Dope Fiend.* Port Townsend, WA: Loompanics, 1998.
Francis Moraes	*The Little Book of Heroin.* Berkeley, CA: Ronin, 2000.
Francis Moraes	*The Little Book of Opium.* Berkeley, CA: Ronin, 2003.

David F. Musto, ed.   *One Hundred Years of Heroin.*
                       Westport, CT: Auburn House, 2002.

Stanton Peele   *Diseasing of America: How We
                       Allowed Recovery Zealots and the
                       Treatment Industry to Convince Us We
                       Are Out of Control.* San Francisco:
                       Jossey-Bass, 1999.

Jerome J. Platt   *Heroin Addiction: Theory, Research,
                       and Treatment; The Addict, the
                       Treatment Process, and Social Control.*
                       Malabar, FL: Krieger, 1995.

Peter Dale Scott   *Drugs, Oil, and War: The United
                       States in Afghanistan, Colombia, and
                       Indochina.* Lanham, MD: Rowman &
                       Littlefield, 2003.

David E. Smith, ed.   *"It's So Good, Don't Even Try It
                       Once": Heroin in Perspective.*
                       Englewood Cliffs, NJ: Prentice-Hall,
                       1972.

Joanne Tatham   *Heroin Kills.* Glasgow, UK: Tramway,
                       2003.

Jack Trimpey   *Rational Recovery: The New Cure for
                       Substance Addiction.* New York:
                       Simon & Schuster, 1996.

Periodicals

Laila Al-Arian   "Pakistani Opium Farmers Riot,"
                      *Washington Report on Middle East
                      Affairs,* June 2004.

Caroline V. Clarke
"Sweet Freedom: Ex-Convict Shakoor Watson Overcame a Heroin Addiction to Build a Thriving Bakery," *Black Enterprise*, June 2003.

Cindy S. Eaves
"Heroin Use Among Female Adolescents: The Role of Partner Influence in Path of Initiation and Route of Administration," *American Journal of Drug and Alcohol Abuse*, February 2004.

Steven Frank
"Fighting Heroin with . . . Heroin," *Time*, February 14, 2005.

Elizabeth Hudson
"Snow Bodies: One Woman's Life on the Streets," *Women's Review of Books*, September 2004.

Curtis Jackson-Jacobs
"Hooked on Heroin: Drugs and Drifters in a Globalized World," *American Journal of Sociology*, March 2005.

Malcolm Jones
"Guns, Money and Dope in the Texas Desert," *Newsweek*, July 25, 2005.

David E. Kaplan, Ilana Ozernoy
"Afghan Fields Are Going to Pot," *U.S. News & World Report*, November 14, 2005.

Susan Mayor
"Value of Prescribing Heroin Is Uncertain," *British Medical Journal*, September 20, 2003.

James D. Medler
"Afghan Heroin: Terrain, Tradition, and Turmoil," *Orbis*, Spring 2005.

Carrie Morantz — "Buprenorphine Mentoring Program for Physicians Debuts Nationwide," *American Family Physician*, August 15, 2005.

Sohail Abdul Nasir — "The Poppy Problem," *Bulletin of the Atomic Scientists*, September/October 2004.

Kate Novack — "Shooting Up Legally Up North," *Time*, July 7, 2003.

Edward T. Pound — "The Terror-Heroin Nexus," *U.S. News & World Report*, February 16, 2004.

Elaine Shannon — "Dope War in Afghanistan," *Time*, September 5, 2005.

Lisa Stein — "Consult an Expert: United States-Colombia Cooperation to Stop Opium Production, Traffic in Afghanistan," *U.S. News & World Report*, March 21, 2005.

Jacob Sullum — "Poppy Flop: The Drug War's High Yields," *Reason*, December 2005.

Jeff A. Taylor — "Supply-Snort Economics," *Reason*, March 2005.

Stephanie Thompson — "Heroin Chic OK, Cocaine Use Not; H&M, Others Drop Kate Moss After Model Notorious for Partying Is Caught Partying," *Advertising Age*, September 26, 2005.

Kenneth T. Walsh, Paul Bedard, David E. Kaplan, and Thomas Omestad — "Iraq, Your Newest Corner Drugstore," *U.S. News & World Report*, June 20, 2005.

James D. Zirin   "You've Got Drugs," *Forbes*, May 23, 2005.

Index